THE
CHILDREN'S
BOOK
OF

MYTHS AND
LEGENDS

THE CHILDREN'S BOOK OF MYTHS AND LEGENDS

RETOLD BY RONNE RANDALL
ILLUSTRATED BY GRAHAM HOWELLS

ARMADILLO

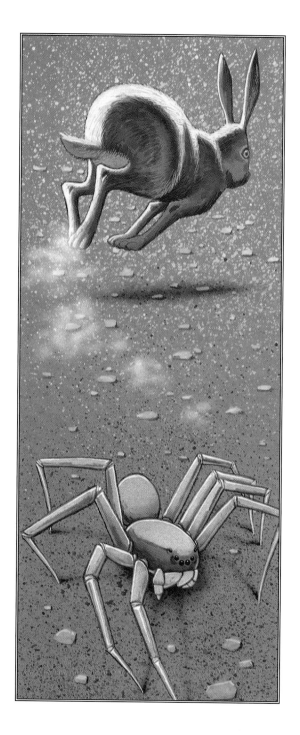

First published in 2001
by Armadillo Books
an imprint of
Bookmart Limited
Registered Number 2372865
Trading as Bookmart Limited
Desford Road, Enderby
Leicester LE9 5AD

ISBN 1-90046-558-2

Produced for Bookmart Limited by
Nicola Baxter
PO Box 215, Framingham Earl,
Norwich NR14 7UR

Designer: Amanda Hawkes
Production designer: Amy Barton

Printed in Singapore

CONTENTS

INTRODUCTION 7

BEGINNINGS 8
Creation from the Waters 10
How the World Came to Be 12
The Great Serpent 14
How the World Began 16
The Dreamtime 18
The Gods Come to Mount Olympus 20
Prometheus and Pandora 22
The Heavens and the World Below 24

THE HEAVENS AND THE
ELEMENTS 26
Utnapishtim and the Flood 28
The Secret Name of Ra 30
Phaeton and the Chariot of the Sun 32
The Moon and the Hare 34
When the Sun Ran Away 36
Tulugaak and the Bag of Light 38

GROWTH AND REBIRTH 40
Isis and Osiris 42
Demeter and Persephone 44
Romulus and Remus 46
Nekumonta and the Healing Waters 48
Miochin and Shakok 50
Uke-Mochi's Secret 52

GODS AND GODDESSES 54
Horus and Set 56
Artemis and Actaeon 58

Arachne the Weaver 60
King Midas and the Golden Touch 62
Idun's Golden Apples 64
Olodumare and Olokun 66
Ananse and the Sky God's Stories 68

LOVE AND MARRIAGE 70
Echo and Narcissus 72
Eros and Psyche 74
Orpheus and Eurydice 76
Paris and the Golden Apple 78
Deirdre of the Sorrows 80
Savitri and Satyavan 82

HEROIC DEEDS 84
Gilgamesh, Enkidu and Humbaba 86
Perseus and Medusa 88
Pegasus and Bellerophon 90
The Twelve Tasks of Hercules 92
Theseus and the Minotaur 94
Daedalus and Icarus 96
Jason and the Golden Fleece 98
The Trojan Horse 100
Odysseus and the Cyclops 102
Sigurd and Fafnir 104
Vainamoinen and the Magic Mill 106
The Sword in the Stone 108
Arthur and Excalibur 110
Gawain and the Green Knight 112
Finn MacCool and the Salmon 114

DEATH AND ENDINGS 116
Gilgamesh, Enkidu and the Bull 118
The Old Man of the Ancients 120
The Death of King Arthur 122
Cuchulainn the Warrior 124
The Battle of Ragnarok 126

Index of Names 128

INTRODUCTION

There are many different kinds of stories. Some are about real people and things, or about people and events that could be real. Other stories feature made-up characters who might do amazing or unbelievable things. Then there are fairy tales and folk tales. These stories are filled with magic and fantasy, and most are very old. But they are not as old as myths.

Myths are the oldest stories of all, and the ones that come from the deepest and most powerful part of the human spirit. They are the stories we have told since the dawn of time, to explain the world around us and to make sense of our place within it.

Closely linked to myths are legends, stories about people who may have once lived, but who have, over the years, grown larger than life. Through the ages, the stories that have been woven around these heroes have glorified them and their deeds to such an extent that they now seem almost like gods.

The myths and legends in this book come from all over the world. They are all filled with adventure, magic, mystery, and the wonders of the human heart and spirit. They are a gift to us from our most distant ancestors, for us to enjoy and treasure for all time.

Long before there were any scientific explanations for how the world was created and how humankind began, people tried to answer these very basic and important questions through myths. These creation stories, therefore, are probably the most ancient myths of all.

Creation myths exist in every culture and religion, and they offer a fascinating glimpse at how the earliest people experienced their world. In hot, dry regions, for example, where water was all-important and life-giving, the Egyptian and Yoruba stories of creation tell of the world emerging from vast, limitless seas. Far to the north, the early Norse people, struggling against their harsh, frozen surroundings, saw the world beginning in endless frost and ice.

In the same way, myths have different explanations about how the first people appeared on Earth. In one Chinese myth, human beings developed from fleas! The Australian Aboriginal and Greek myths retold here tell how humankind was formed from earth or clay, a tradition that also exists in Jewish and Christian creation beliefs.

What all these myths have in common is the belief that the world was created through the will of a divine being (or beings), and that humans were part of this creation.

BEGINNINGS

CREATION
FROM THE WATERS

Egyptian myths tell how everything was created from the water that covered the earth. This reflects the way that everything in Egypt was made possible by the waters of the Nile.

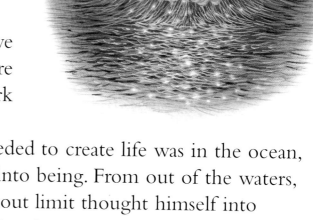

Before the world as we know it existed, there was only a great, dark sea, called the ocean of Nun.

Everything that was needed to create life was in the ocean, but it needed to be brought into being. From out of the waters, a god whose power was without limit thought himself into existence. He called himself Ra, the sun god.

As he breathed out, Ra made the air and called it Shu. From his saliva, he made moisture, which he named Tefnut. Ra made an island to stand on and began to call out of Nun all the living things of the world. Plants, birds and animals came into being as he called their names.

Meanwhile, Shu and Tefnut had gone out into the world and had children of their own. They were called Geb, the earth, and Nut, the sky. They were always together.

But Shu, the air, blew between them, forcing them apart. Nut's body arched, so that her hands and feet stood at the ends of the earth but there was room for the air to blow beneath her, just as it still blows between the earth and sky today.

Nut became the mother of creation. She gave birth to the stars that shine at night. Each evening, she swallowed the sun. In the morning, she gave birth to it again, so that light could shine over Egypt once more.

And Nut gave birth to the great gods of Egypt: Osiris, the lord of life; Horus with his falcon head; Set, lord of the desert; the great goddess Isis; and Nephthys, Queen of the Dead.

HOW THE WORLD
CAME TO BE

In some versions of this myth, from the Yoruba people of Nigeria, Obatala gets drunk and cannot do his job, so Olodumare sends another god to create the land instead. However, Olodumare later forgives Obatala and allows him to shape the bodies of people and animals.

At the beginning of time, when there was only heaven above, and water below, the god Obatala looked out over the waters. "That vast sea is too empty," he told Olodumare, the chief of all the gods. "There should be dry places here and there, where creatures can live and look up to see the heavens."

"You are right, Obatala," said Olodumare. "And you should be the one to create the land and shape the creatures to live there."

With the help of the other gods, Obatala fashioned a golden chain long enough to reach down from the heavens. Then Orunmila, the god of prophecy, gave him a sack, which held a snail shell filled with sand, a hen, and a palm nut.

Throwing the sack over his shoulder, Obatala hung the chain from a corner of the sky and climbed down. When he was just above the water, he took out the snail shell and poured out the sand. Then he let the hen go. As soon as a pile of sand fell on the water, the hen began scratching about in it, scattering it everywhere. Wherever a bit of sand fell, a patch of dry land spread out.

Obatala buried a palm nut in the sand, and a tall tree sprang up, scattering more nuts around it, which also sprang up into trees. Then Obatala mixed the sand with water and shaped it into figures.

His work done, Obatala called out to Olodumare, the Creator, to breathe life into the figures he had made. This Olodumare did, and the figures became living people and animals, who spread out over the newly created earth.

THE GREAT SERPENT

The image of a coiled serpent with its tail in its mouth, representing eternity and immortality, appears in the myths of many different cultures around the world. This myth comes from the Fon people of West Africa.

Nanu-Buluku, the one god and the creator, who is neither male nor female, existed before everything and everyone.

Aido-Hwedo, the great serpent, was Nanu-Buluku's servant, and he carried the creator everywhere in his mouth, turning and curving and twisting and winding and bending this way and that. And so the earth's valleys and rivers turn and curve and wind and twist and bend this way and that.

When Nanu-Buluku had created the earth, it was so heavy from the weight of all the mountains and trees and rocks and creatures that it was in danger of toppling over! The creator asked Aido-Hwedo to coil himself beneath it and hold it up.

But the earth was fiery hot, and Aido-Hwedo cannot stand heat. The creator made the oceans to keep the serpent cool, and that is where Aido-Hwedo has lived since the beginning of time—deep beneath the sea, holding his tail in his mouth.

Now, sometimes Aido-Hwedo has to move around to make himself more comfortable. When he does that, the earth shifts and moves around, too, and we have earthquakes.

Red monkeys live beneath the sea, and Nanu-Buluku gave them the job of making the iron bars that the great serpent eats. But one day the monkeys' supply of iron will run out, and then Aido-Hwedo will have nothing to eat. His hunger will grow and grow, until he starts to chew his own tail. Then he will thrash about so much that the earth will fall over and slip into the sea.

And that will be that!

HOW THE WORLD BEGAN

This Chinese myth has its source in the ancient belief system called Taoism, which says that harmony in the universe comes from balancing opposites such as male and female and good and evil. The name for all these opposing forces is Yin (dark) and Yang (light), represented by this symbol:

1 n the Great Beginning, there was only Chaos, made up of two kinds of energy, Yin and Yang. Chaos was held within an enormous egg, along with a divine being called Pan Ku.

Chaos fought with itself, until eventually the egg burst, and Chaos escaped. Yin, the cold, light energy, drifted up to become the heavens. The warm, heavy energy, Yang, sank down and became the earth.

Yin and Yang still wanted to fight with one another, so Pan Ku had to stand between them and push them apart. As he did this, he grew and grew and grew. At last, after eighteen thousand years, Pan Ku was an enormous giant, and heaven and earth were so distant from one another that they could not harm each other.

Pan Ku's work was finished. He was very, very old, and very, very tired. So the giant lay down upon the earth he had created and prepared to die.

As he died, a miracle happened. Pan Ku's hands and feet became the four quarters of our earth. His head turned into the mountains that rise up from the earth, and his eyes became the sun and moon. A thousand different plants and trees grew from his skin and hair. His breath was transformed into the wind and clouds, and his voice into the rolling thunder from the heavens. His teeth, bones and marrow became the metals, rocks and precious stones within the earth, and his sweat turned into flowing rivers. Last of all, the fleas and lice that leaped and crept all over his hairy body became the human beings who have lived on Pan Ku's earth ever since.

THE DREAMTIME

The Aboriginal people of Australia have a close and sacred relationship with the land, as this creation myth shows. Australian Aboriginals still feel closely connected to the Ancestor spirits, and their Dreamtime journey is acted out as part of Aboriginal religious ceremonies.

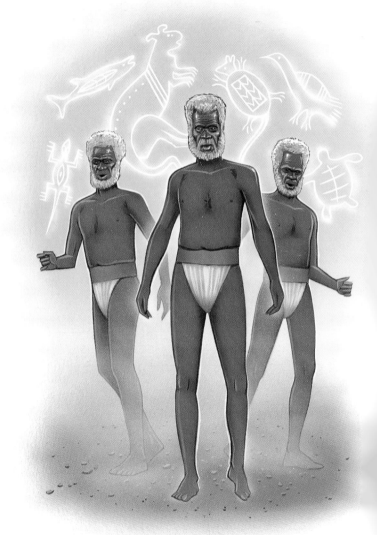

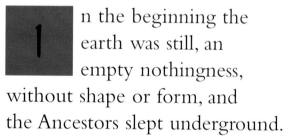**1** n the beginning the earth was still, an empty nothingness, without shape or form, and the Ancestors slept underground.

Then the Dreamtime came, when the Ancestors rose up and began to walk the earth, singing as they went. They sang the names of animals, of trees, of grasses and flowers and birds. And as they sang each name, what they sang came into being. The earth came to life.

On their wanderings, the Ancestors found shapeless heaps lying about, heavy, muddy, half-made creatures that could not move or breathe—they could only lie there, lifeless.

The Ancestors fashioned knives from stones, and with these knives they carved heads and faces, arms and hands, legs and feet. From the half-made creatures, they made fully formed human beings, and breathed life into them. These humans became the Ancestors' spirit children.

The Ancestors gave the earth to their spirit children, and taught them how to live with the plants and animals, and how to care for them and for the land that they had been given.

Now their work was finished, and the Ancestors went back to sleep. Some of them went back underground, some of them went up to the sky, and others became rocks and trees.

The paths the Ancestors walked back then, in the Dreamtime, were called Songlines, after the songs they sang as they wandered. The Songlines became sacred trails, and the traces the Ancestors left behind—the trees, the rocks, the waterholes—are sacred, too, for all time.

THE GODS
COME TO MOUNT OLYMPUS

To the ancient Greeks, the gods were real, and their myths were treated as history. Some ancient Greeks even claimed to be descendants of the gods. Mount Olympus, the home of the gods, is a real mountain in northern Greece, which looks high enough to touch the heavens.

Gaia, Mother Earth, created the earth and all its mountains, rivers, deserts, and oceans. Then she joined with Uranus, the heavens, to make all the animals and birds that roamed the earth and flew in the air.

Gaia and Uranus had twelve children—six sons and six daughters. These were the Titans, the first gods and goddesses. Cronus, the youngest Titan, hated his father and fought bitterly with him, until he finally took over his throne. But then Cronus began to worry that his own children would turn against him in turn. So each time his wife, Rhea, bore a child, he devoured it.

Rhea, heartbroken at losing her children and furious at Cronus's cruelty, went to Gaia for help. The next time Rhea was expecting a child, Gaia took her away to a secret island to have her baby. She named the child Zeus and hid him in a cave, safe from his father. Rhea took a rock back for Cronus to swallow, and he never knew the difference.

Zeus grew up strong and powerful, and went home to confront his father. He gave Cronus a potion to make him cough up the children he had swallowed. Then, with his brothers and sisters, Zeus went up to Mount Olympus.

From their home in the clouds, Zeus and his brothers and sisters waged war against the Titans. Finally the Titans were defeated. Zeus was now lord of Mount Olympus and master of his brothers and sisters, who themselves became the gods and goddesses who ruled the world.

PROMETHEUS
AND PANDORA

Pandora's name means "all gifted" because each of the gods and goddesses gave her a gift when she was created. She is the first mortal woman in Greek mythology, and is often compared with Eve, the first woman in the Bible.

During the war between Zeus and the Titans, two Titans fought on Zeus's side—Prometheus and his brother, Epimetheus. When Zeus became lord of Mount Olympus, he asked Prometheus to make some mortal beings. So Prometheus took clay from the earth and shaped it into people.

Mother Earth had given Prometheus a basket filled with gifts to be given to human beings and to the animals she herself had created. Epimetheus begged to be allowed to give out some of the gifts, and though Prometheus knew his brother was foolish, he agreed.

Epimetheus immediately began giving gifts to the animals—strength and stealth, swiftness and courage. He gave them wings and claws and hard shells for protection. Soon there was almost nothing left in the basket for the human beings! So Prometheus decided to give them something very special. With the help of the goddess Athene, he went up to the sun and brought down fire for humankind.

When Zeus discovered what Prometheus had done, he was enraged. He decided to punish the Titan by causing trouble for humanity. He created a woman named Pandora, and asked each of the gods to give her a gift. Aphrodite gave her beauty, Hermes gave her a quick wit, and so on. Zeus presented the woman to Epimetheus. He knew that Prometheus would be too clever to accept such a gift!

In his house, Epimetheus had a jar in which all kinds of horrible things were stored—illness and wickedness, poverty and misery, warfare and cruelty. He told Pandora that she must never, ever open this jar. Of course, that only made her curious, and one day she went to have a look.

Instantly, all the horrible things flew out of the jar. Pandora quickly put the lid back, but it was too late. The horrors were already scattered over the earth. Only one thing was left—hope, which has helped people endure the rest ever since.

THE HEAVENS
AND THE WORLD BELOW

Yggdrasil, the tree that supports the universe in Norse mythology, was said to have sprung from the body of Ymir, the Frost Giant. Ymir's body was believed to remain beneath the tree, and every now and then he tries to shake it off, causing the earth to shudder and quake.

At the beginning of time there was only frost and ice, and Ymir, the Frost Giant, and Audumla, his cow, were the only two beings to inhabit this frozen expanse. One day, Audumla was licking some ice when suddenly a hair appeared. The next day an entire head appeared, and the day after that a whole being emerged. This was Bor, the first god.

Bor and his wife, Bestla, created three more gods: Odin, Vili, and Ve, who slew the giant Ymir. From Ymir's flesh, the gods made the earth. His bones became the mountains, his skull became the heavens, and Ymir's blood became the dark seas. Then Odin placed the moon and the sun in the heavens, and trees and plants began to grow.

But the world still seemed incomplete, so Odin and his brothers took two trees and made a man and a woman, whom they called Aske and Embla. Then, from Ymir's eyebrows, the gods made a world called Midgard, which they gave to Aske and Embla as their home. These two became the ancestors of the entire human race.

The gods were now ready to give order to the universe, and they divided it into three levels. At the highest level was Asgard, the home of the gods, reached by a rainbow bridge. Below that was Midgard, home of human beings; Jotunheim, the land of the giants; and Nidavellir and Svartalfheim, where dwarves and elves lived. At the bottom were Niflheim and Hel, the homes of the dead. Supporting everything was Yggdrasil, a mighty ash tree. Yggdrasil's trunk runs through the heart of the universe, and its roots and branches spread throughout all creation.

O ur ancestors found the powerful and ever-changing patterns of the natural world awe-inspiring and mysterious. How did the wondrous lights of the sun, stars and moon come to be? What could explain uncontrollable events such as eclipses, or rains so heavy that they caused floods? The myths in this section all focus on these extraordinary experiences.

The most important heavenly body is, of course, the sun, and it is the subject of several of the myths in this section— from the Greek myth of Phaeton, which depicts the sun as a fiery force that has the power to change the face of the earth, to the Inuit myth in which the raven god Tulugaak releases light from a bag to rescue the world from darkness.

Myths deal with the power of the heavens to release harmful forces, too, such as the torrential rains in the ancient Mesopotamian myth of Utnapishtim. The story of a deluge, followed by a flood that covers the earth, is found in many cultures around the world. Though there may not ever have been such a flood, ancient people might well have seen their own land as the entire world, so any major flood would have been experienced as total destruction.

These myths still speak powerfully to us today—after all, the weather and climate still have a huge effect on us.

THE HEAVENS AND THE ELEMENTS

UTNAPISHTIM
AND THE FLOOD

Cultures all over the world
have a story about a great
flood in their mythology.
This tale, from the ancient
Mesopotamian Epic of
Gilgamesh, has striking
similarities to the Biblical
account of Noah and his ark.

After human beings were created, the earth was peaceful
for many years. But Ishtar, goddess of love and war,
made people fight with one another. There was so much
noise and confusion that the gods could not rest.

Enlil, god of the air, decided to send a rainstorm that would
flood the earth and destroy the unruly people. He made the
other gods promise not to warn the people of the coming disaster.

But Ea, god of water, had one good and faithful servant,
Utnapishtim, whom he wanted to save. So that he would not
break his promise to Enlil, Ea whispered a warning to the reeds
that grew by the banks of the River Euphrates. Then the reeds
whispered the secret to Utnapishtim while he slept.

Utnapishtim was wise and heeded his dream. He built a boat big enough to hold all his family, and one male and one female of every living creature on earth.

The storm came, and rain fell for six days and six nights. All the world was drowned. But all who sailed in Utnapishtim's boat were safe.

On the seventh day, the rain stopped, and Utnapishtim's boat came to rest at the top of Mount Nisir. Utnapishtim sent out a dove, and it returned. The next day he sent out a swallow. It too came back. On the third day, Utnapishtim sent out a raven. When it did not return, Utnapishtim knew it had found a dry place to land. Joyfully, he and his family, and all the animals, left the boat.

Enlil and Ea took Utnapishtim and his wife by the hand, and touched their foreheads and said, "You are no longer ordinary humans. Now you are like the gods—you will live forever, and be mother and father of all the people to come."

THE SECRET NAME OF RA

To the ancient Egyptians, the sun's journey across the heavens represented the life cycle, from birth at sunrise through old age and death at sunset. Each night Ra, the sun god, would battle the demons of the Underworld before being reborn again at dawn.

The great god Ra, who created the world and named the gods, had his own hidden, secret name. As long as he kept it secret, nothing and no one could harm him.

After he had created people, Ra himself took the form of a man to rule over Egypt. Eventually, like all men, Ra grew old and frail, and sometimes he dribbled, as old men do. Yet he was still the most powerful of all the gods.

Isis, the wisest goddess, longed to be as powerful as Ra, so she thought of a way to make him tell her his secret name. Wherever Ra went, Isis followed him. When he dribbled, she collected his saliva and mixed it with earth to make mud. From this mud she made a cobra, which sprang up and bit Ra, sending its venom through his veins.

Ra was in agony. He cried out, "Something has bitten me—something not of my creation."

Isis drew near. "I can heal you," she said, "but only if you tell me your secret name."

"I am Khephera in the morning, Ra at noon, and Atum in the evening," said Ra. "I am the Maker of Heaven and Earth, the Builder of Mountains and the Creator of Rivers…."

But Isis knew that none of these was his most secret name.

At last Ra could bear the pain no longer. He asked Isis to swear that she would never tell the secret name to any god or mortal, but would keep it within her heart forever. Isis swore, and the knowledge of Ra's secret name passed from his heart into hers.

"By the name which I know," she said, "let the poison go from Ra!"

The pain vanished at once. But Ra could not rule upon the earth any longer. Instead, he took his place in the heavens, to travel across the sky each day, and cross each night into the Underworld, where he carried the souls of the dead safely to their home.

PHAETON
AND THE CHARIOT OF THE SUN

Helios, the Greek sun god in this myth, was the son of a Titan and one of the first Olympian gods. In later myths, he is replaced as sun god by Apollo, who was also the god of archery, music and prophecy.

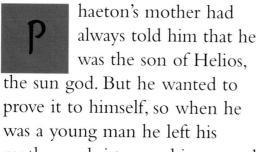

P haeton's mother had always told him that he was the son of Helios, the sun god. But he wanted to prove it to himself, so when he was a young man he left his mother and sisters and journeyed to the east to find his father.

At last Phaeton came to the palace of the sun and saw Helios before him, dazzling on his golden throne.

"Welcome, my son," said Helios. His words and smile left no doubt in Phaeton's mind that this was indeed his father.

"My son," said Helios, "is there some gift I can give you?"

"There is one thing, Father," said Phaeton eagerly. "May I drive your chariot across the sky?"

Helios's face darkened. "The horses are spirited," he said, "and the ride is treacherous. The task is far too dangerous for anyone but me."

But Phaeton begged and pleaded, and at last Helios gave in. He tried to tell his son how to guide the horses and which route to take, but Phaeton was too excited to pay attention.

As soon as he took the reins, Phaeton knew that he had made a terrible mistake. The horses bolted forward, out of control, and the chariot hurtled wildly through the skies—sometimes so close to the earth that cities were set ablaze and grasslands turned to deserts, and sometimes so far away that whole regions turned to ice.

Zeus saw what was happening and knew there was only one way to end the catastrophe. He hurled a thunderbolt at Phaeton, causing him to fall from the chariot and plunge to his death. Only then could Helios guide the chariot home.

THE MOON
AND THE HARE

The Hare is a mischievous trickster figure in myths from many parts of Africa. In the stories told by African slaves in America, Hare became the wily and cunning character known as Brer Rabbit.

E very night, as she moved across the sky, the Moon Goddess looked down at the people on earth. She saw that they were frightened and sad, because they knew that one day they would die.

The Moon Goddess decided to give the people a great gift, one that would make them like the gods—the gift of immortality. "Go down to earth," she told steadfast Spider, "and tell the people: 'Just as the moon dies and then rises again, so shall you.'"

Slowly and carefully, Spider crawled down the moonbeams to earth. As he crept along, he met Hare, who asked where he was going.

"I am taking a message from the Moon Goddess to the people of the earth," said Spider, and he repeated it to Hare.

"But you're so slow!" said Hare. "The people will be old by the time you reach them. I'll take the message for you!" And before Spider could stop him, Hare had raced off.

Hare was swift, but he was also very careless. He left out an important part of the message. He told the people: "The Moon Goddess says, 'Just as the moon dies, so shall you!'"

This made the people even sadder. The Spider was too late to help. What was done could not be undone.

When the Moon Goddess learned what Hare had done, she was so angry that she smacked him and split his lip. Hare ran away—and he is still running, to this day.

WHEN THE SUN RAN AWAY

Amaterasu, the chief goddess of the Shinto religion, is traditionally believed to be the ancestor of Japan's emperors. Millions of people visit her shrine at Ise every year, and Japan is called "the land of the rising sun" as a tribute to her.

W hen the god Izanagi divided his kingdom among his children, he gave Susanowo the oceans; he gave Tsuki Yomi the night sky, with the moon and the stars; and Amaterasu was given the sun and the heavens by day. She brought light and warmth to the world, and made everything grow.

Susanowo grew jealous of Amaterasu, so he churned up the oceans and created storms to trouble the world. Winds howled over the earth, destroying fields and trees and ruining crops. Amaterasu was so angry and upset that she hid in a cave and refused to come out.

Without Amaterasu's warmth and light, the world turned cold and dark, and evil and chaos took over.

The other gods knew the world would be destroyed unless Amaterasu came back, so they began trying to lure her out. First they hung a magic mirror right outside her cave. Then they put jewels in the trees, and lit bonfires. Finally, Uzume, the goddess of dancing and merriment, did a whirling, mad dance that made all the other gods roar with laughter.

From within the cave, Amaterasu asked what all the noise was about. "We have found a goddess even more radiant than you," the others told her. "We're having a party to celebrate!"

Of course, Amaterasu was curious. When she looked out, she was captivated by her own reflection in the magic mirror. Then the gods grabbed Amaterasu's hand and pulled her out. They blocked up the cave so that she could never go back in.

Amaterasu returned to her place in the heavens, bringing light and warmth and new life to the land, and she has never gone away again.

TULUGAAK
AND THE BAG OF LIGHT

This story comes from the Inuit (Eskimo) people of northern Canada and Alaska. Tulugaak, or Raven, is the Inuit creator god, who often takes human form to bring gifts to the people he has created.

L ong ago, when the world was new, there was no sun and no moon. The earth was always in darkness.

In those times there was a young woman who lived with her father near the edge of the sea. One day, the girl saw a feather in the air. She had never seen a feather before, and she opened her mouth in surprise. In an instant, the feather had floated into her mouth and she had swallowed it.

Nine months later, the young woman had a baby. It had a human body, but its mouth was a raven's bill, so she named it Tulugaak, which means Raven.

High on a wall of the house there hung a big, blown-up bag made of animal skin that belonged to the woman's father. He had told his daughter never to touch it. But one day the baby was so restless and fretful that she took down the bag and gave it to him to play with. As soon as he had it, he stopped crying.

Gleefully, the baby rolled the bag along the floor and threw it into the air. Then, all at once, his sharp beak burst the bag.

Suddenly brightness filled the air—not just in the house, but everywhere in the world. Light streamed from the sky and poured over everything. And the sky stayed light until evening, when it began to grow dark again.

That night, the girl's father scolded her for giving the baby the bag of light. And when it next grew light again, Tulugaak had disappeared. But the light that had escaped from the animal-skin bag stayed, and from then on there was both light and darkness in the world.

The earliest people saw that the changing seasons brought about miraculous events. Plants died, and reappeared the following year. Seeds, which seemed such tiny, lifeless objects, could be buried in the ground, then burst into life. Why did this happen?

The Greek myth of Demeter and her daughter Persephone, and the Native American story of Miochin and Shakok both suggest reasons for the way that winter is followed by spring and summer year after year. We can imagine that tales like tales were told around the fire in the depths of winter, when hope that the sun would shine again on the world one day began to fade, and food stocks were getting low.

People, too, go through changes as they grow and age. We all begin as helpless babies. Could it be, our ancestors wondered, that we die and are reborn, pass and come again, like tiny seeds or the recurring seasons?

In a world that often seemed violent and beyond the control of human beings, ideas of natural cycles and renewal must have been a great comfort. The Japanese myth of Uke-mochi tells that even the anger of the storm god Susanowo cannot destroy the goddess who supplies food to people on Earth. Even in death, her body brings forth grains, rice, and beans to nourish humankind.

GROWTH
AND
REBIRTH

ISIS AND OSIRIS

To the ancient Egyptians, the yearly flood of the Nile was necessary for survival, for without it no crops would grow. Isis, whose tears bring about the flood, became the Egyptians' most important goddess. She continued to be worshipped long after belief in the other Egyptian gods and goddesses faded.

The god Osiris became the king of Egypt, with Isis as his queen. Osiris ruled wisely, giving his people laws and teaching them to worship the gods. He also taught them how to farm the land and bring crops out of the earth. He was loved by everyone, except his jealous brother Set.

Determined to destroy his brother, Set built a beautiful casket, just the right size to fit Osiris.

Then Set held a banquet, and invited his guests to lie in the casket. "Whoever fits it exactly may have it as a gift," said Set.

Of course, only Osiris fit into the casket exactly. As soon as his brother was inside, Set bolted down the lid. He flung the casket into the Nile, and it drifted out to sea, where Osiris died.

Heartbroken, Isis set out to look for her husband's coffin. After many months, she found it in a palace in the city of Byblos.

Isis brought the coffin back to Egypt and hid it in a marsh, but Set soon discovered it. Enraged, he hacked Osiris's body to pieces and scattered them all over Egypt.

Once again, Isis searched tirelessly until she had found nearly all the pieces of her husband's body. She put them together, and brought him back to life for just one night, when she conceived their son Horus. Then Osiris went down to the Underworld.

But every year, after Set's burning hatred has scorched the land, Isis's tears for her dead husband cause the Nile to swell and flood the parched earth. Then Osiris comes to life again, bringing grain from the ground to feed the people he loves.

DEMETER
AND PERSEPHONE

This ancient Greek myth explains the changing seasons and the growth of plants. Demeter, the goddess of grain, was known to the Romans as Ceres, and we get the word "cereal" from her name.

T here was a time when the world was warm and sunny all year, trees bore fruit continually, and grain grew again as soon as it was cut down. The goddess Demeter ruled over all these growing things, and she had a daughter named Kore, which means "maiden" in Greek.

One day Kore was out gathering flowers when the earth opened up and Hades, lord of the Underworld, rose up in his chariot. He grabbed the screaming Kore and pulled her down, into the depths of the Underworld.

When Demeter learned that her daughter had become the bride of Hades and was now named Persephone, she stormed and raged. The earth became cold and barren.

At last Zeus persuaded Hades to send Persephone back, but Hades had one condition—Persephone could return only if she had not eaten anything that grew in the Underworld. Persephone hadn't eaten anything, but she had sucked six pomegranate seeds.

"Then she will have to remain in the Underworld for six months of every year," Hades declared. "For the other six months, she may return to Demeter."

So for six months every year, when Persephone is in the Underworld, the earth is cold and wintry. But when she returns to her mother, warmth and life come with her, and the earth brings forth its bounty once more.

ROMULUS AND REMUS

The Romans believed that after he died, Romulus was taken to heaven in a whirlwind by his father, the god Mars. There he became a god himself, known as Quirinus. One of the seven hills on which Rome was built, the Quirinal, takes its name from him.

Numitor, the king of the ancient city of Alba Longa, in what is now Italy, had a daughter named Rhea Silvia. He also had a jealous brother named Amulius, who imprisoned him and took over his kingdom. Amulius forced Rhea Silvia to become a vestal virgin, a young woman who was forbidden to marry or have children.

But Mars, the god of war, came to visit Rhea Silvia one night, and nine months later she gave birth to twin boys, whom she called Romulus and Remus. Amulius, frightened that the boys would overthrow him when they grew up, threw them into the River Tiber along with their mother.

Rhea Silvia drowned, but the boys drifted to shore and were found by a she-wolf, who carried them off and cared for them tenderly, suckling them as she would her own cubs. The boys grew strong and sturdy in her care. One day a shepherd named Faustulus, who had worked for their grandfather King Numitor, found the boys running wild in the forest. He knew at once who they were, and he took them home and raised them as his own sons.

When Romulus and Remus were young men, Faustulus told them who they were and what had happened to them. Together, they killed their treacherous uncle and released their grandfather so he could reclaim his throne.

Then the boys decided to build a city on the River Tiber, at the place where they had come ashore as babies. But they argued about which of them should rule over it, and in the argument Romulus killed his brother. He became king of the new city, and named it after himself—Rome.

NEKUMONTA
AND THE HEALING WATERS

This story comes from the Iroquois people, who lived in what is now northern New York State. Manitou, the Great Spirit, sometimes called Kitchi Manito, is the supreme god of several Native American tribes from around the Great Lakes.

There was once a strong and wise young hunter named Nekumonta, who loved animals and treated them kindly. He never killed an animal unless it was needed for food or clothing.

One winter a deadly plague broke out in Nekumonta's village. Many people died, and Nekumonta's beloved wife Shanewis fell ill. "Surely Manitou, the Great Spirit, has given us some herb or plant that will heal this terrible sickness," thought Nekumonta. "I must go out and find it."

For three long days, Nekumonta searched in the forest for healing herbs. But not a stalk nor a leaf nor even a blade of grass could he find in the frozen ground. At last, exhausted and weak, Nekumonta lay down to sleep beneath some trees. As the animals and birds watched over him, they remembered his kindness and begged Manitou to help their friend.

Manitou heard their pleas, and sent Nekumonta a dream in which his wife Shanewis sang to him and turned into a waterfall. "Seek me," the water sang to Nekumonta, "to save your people."

When Nekumonta woke up, he could hear the ground beneath his feet singing. "Set us free," it sang, "and your people will live!"

Frantically, Nekumonta began digging, and soon a bubbling spring rippled up. When Nekumonta washed in it, his aching limbs grew strong again. He filled a clay jar with the healing water, and carried it back to his village. Hurrying to where Shanewis lay sleeping, he put some of the water on her parched lips. When she woke, she was well again.

All the people of the village drank the water, and the plague left them forever. From then on, Nekumonta was known as Chief of the Healing Waters, the one who brought Manitou's gift of healing to his people.

MIOCHIN
AND SHAKOK

This story comes from the Laguna and Acoma people, Native Americans who still live in settlements called pueblos in New Mexico. According to tradition, they originally lived farther north but migrated south because of cold and famine. This myth may be a way of retelling that part of their history.

When Co-chin, the daughter of a chief, married Shakok, the Winter Spirit, the days grew cold and frosty, and the corn stopped growing. Co-chin and her people had nothing to eat but cactus and wild plants.

One day, when Co-chin was out gathering cactus leaves, she met a tall young man wearing leggings made of green moss and a shirt woven from corn silk. In his hand was an ear of ripe corn.

"Why are you gathering cactus leaves?" the man asked Co-chin. When she told him, he gave her the corn. "I will come back tomorrow," he said, "and bring enough to feed all your people."

"Where will you get it?" she asked him.

"From my home in the south," replied the man. "I am Miochin, the Summer Spirit, and in my home corn grows and flowers bloom all year long."

"I wish I could go there with you," said Co-chin.

"Wouldn't your husband, Shakok, be angry?" asked Miochin.

"Shakok is always angry and cold and bitter," said Co-chin. "Please come with me and convince him to let me go."

Of course, Shakok was furious when he came home and found Miochin there. He challenged him to a fight, to decide whom Co-chin would live with.

Shakok unleashed snow and hail and sleet, but Miochin's blazing heat melted the ice and turned Shakok's cold blasts to warm breezes. At last the two called a truce and decided that Co-chin would live with both of them—for half a year each. When she is with Shakok, the world is cold and icy. But then she goes to live with Miochin, and there is sunshine and tall corn grows in the warm earth.

UKE-MOCHI'S
SECRET

This is one of a number of Shinto myths from Japan that portray the storm god Susanowo flying into a destructive rage. His headstrong manner so upset the other gods and goddesses that eventually they banished him from heaven and sent him to live in the Underworld.

Wusanowo, the god of the oceans, was wandering across the land one day when he met Uke-mochi, the goddess who provided food for all the other gods and goddesses.

"Uke-mochi," he said, "you must be very clever to create all the rice and fish and seaweed we eat. What is your secret?"

"It will not be a secret if I tell you," said Uke-mochi. "Perhaps you should not know."

"I must know!" said Susanowo, growing impatient. "Tell me!"

Uke-mochi knew what a violent temper Susanowo had, and she didn't want him to get angry. "All right," she said. "Come and see me this evening, and we will have a meal together. Then you will see how I create food."

That evening, Susanowo watched as Uke-mochi turned toward a field and coughed. Out of her mouth poured a stream of rice. Then she turned to the sea and coughed again. Out of her mouth poured a stream of fish, and lacy fronds of seaweed.

Susanowo was furious. "I have never seen anything so disgusting!" he roared. "How dare you offer me food that comes from within your own body!" As he raged and bellowed, the winds blew up, the sky shook with thunder and the sea rose up in mighty waves. Then Susanowo, overcome with anger, killed Uke-mochi and cut off her head.

But Uke-mochi's power did not die. As her body joined the earth, new life sprang out of it—rice and beans and grains of all kinds. Susanowo's gentle sister, Amaterasu, the sun goddess, took all this food and gave it to human beings, and it nourishes them to this day.

The belief that supernatural beings affect what happens here on Earth is a very ancient one. In some myths and legends there is one all-powerful spirit. In others, whole families of competing gods and goddesses are identified with different aspects of human lives or natural forces.

Although gods and goddesses are supernatural, they often have very human characteristics. Greek myths, in particular, are full of gods and goddesses who are jealous, proud, vain or driven by the desire for revenge. They may also fall in love with humans, creating even more confusion here on Earth.

Scandinavian mythology also has a family of gods, including some who play tricks on each other and ordinary humans. The people who first told these stories knew only too well that life itself often seems to play tricks on us. Could it be, they wondered, that some supernatural being was the cause?

Although gods and goddesses are seen as very powerful, they can be surprised by ordinary earth-dwellers. In the African Ananse stories, the simple spider surprises the sky god by rising to his challenge.

Although the gods and goddesses in these stories may not always have the best interests of humans at heart, they do always have something to teach us about life and how we live it.

GODS
AND
GODDESSES

HORUS
and SET

Crocodiles, who were associated with the water god Sebek, were both feared and worshipped by the ancient Egyptians. In this story crocodiles help Set do battle against Horus, but in other myths, they are helpful to Isis and Osiris and protectors of Horus.

orus was determined to avenge his father's death and to take back the Egyptian throne from his wicked uncle Set. So he challenged Set to a battle.

With the help of Thoth, the god of magic, Horus transformed himself into a winged sun-disk. When Set's army arrived on the battlefield, Horus flew straight to the sun. From there he looked down so fiercely on the soldiers that they were half-blinded by his brightness. They became confused, and each man thought he was standing beside an enemy. The soldiers lashed out and began to kill one another. In the chaos and confusion, Set ran to hide.

The survivors of the battle fled to the River Nile, where they became crocodiles and hippopotamuses. Horus attacked them with a spear that Thoth had given him, and managed to slay them all.

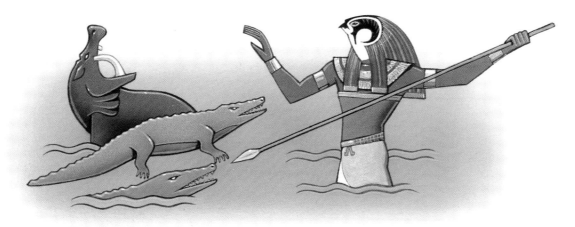

Set, consumed with rage, sent out a servant in disguise to meet Horus. Horus, thinking it was Set himself, killed the man and cut his body into pieces, just as Set had done with his father.

Meanwhile Set took the form of a snake and lay in wait for Horus. But Horus escaped his attack.

The battles and conflicts went on for years. Many times Set tried to trick Horus, but each time Horus was victorious. At last, after eighty years of fighting, Ra proclaimed Horus the winner, and he took his rightful place on the throne of Egypt. Horus was the last god to reign as king, but his spirit entered every earthly pharaoh who ruled after him.

ARTEMIS
AND ACTAEON

Although this is a Greek myth, the most famous version of it is the one told by the Roman poet Ovid in a collection of poetic stories called *Metamorphoses*. Artemis (whom the Romans called Diana) was the goddess of the moon as well as of the hunt.

Deep in a forest, there was a cave sacred to Artemis, the goddess of the hunt. Beside the cave was a spring of pure, clear water, and it was here that Artemis came to bathe and refresh herself when she was weary of hunting.

One day, Artemis arrived at her sacred spring with her nymphs, the woodland spirits who looked after her. She handed them her bow and her arrows, and removed her robe and sandals. Then she stepped naked into the sparkling spring.

Not far away, a young prince named Actaeon was hunting with his friends. But he grew tired of the chase, and left the others to wander through the forest with his dogs.

All at once he came upon the spring where Artemis was bathing. He could not take his gaze from the beautiful woman before him.

Artemis was horrified. To be seen naked by a mortal man was too much for her sense of modesty and dignity to bear.

Quickly, she splashed water in Actaeon's face. "Now go and tell the world that you have seen Artemis naked!" she said. Actaeon felt something strange at the top of his head—and saw that his body was covered in a hairy hide. Artemis had turned him into a stag, complete with a fine set of antlers!

Shocked and terrified, Actaeon tried to run away. But his dogs, seeing a running stag, chased after him, as they had been trained to do. "I am Actaeon, your master!" he wanted to tell them. But of course, stags cannot speak. His own hounds brought Actaeon down and buried their teeth in his throat, ending his life.

ARACHNE
THE WEAVER

In this fateful weaving contest, the Greek goddess Athene wove scenes showing what happened to disrespectful humans who disobeyed the gods. Arachne's tapestry, however, showed gods and goddesses misbehaving—which added fuel to Athene's anger.

A rachne was a young girl who was so gifted at weaving that people came great distances to watch her work and admire her exquisite tapestries. "Athene herself must have taught you," they said to her. For it was the goddess Athene who had taught human beings the craft of weaving.

"Not even Athene is good enough to be my teacher," said Arachne scornfully. "In fact, I wish I could challenge her to a weaving contest, as I'm sure I would win."

When Athene heard about Arachne's boasting, she decided to visit the girl disguised as an old woman.

"Your talents are great," she told Arachne, "but do not be so arrogant as to think you are better than a goddess."

Arachne ignored the warning. "I am every bit as good as I say I am," she said.

The goddess threw off her disguise. "Have your wish, then, foolish maiden," she said. "Let the contest begin!"

The onlookers gasped. Even Arachne turned pale. But it was too late to back down. Both Arachne and Athene worked swiftly and gracefully. Breathtaking tapestries flowed from their fingers. Athene was pleased with her work but when she saw how splendid Arachne's tapestry was, she flew into a rage. She struck Arachne on the forehead, saying, "You and your descendants will remember this day, for you will weave and spin for all eternity!"

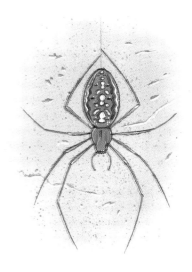

Arachne began to shrivel and shrink, until she was as small as a pea. Her slim fingers became eight slender legs, which scurried across the floor and up the wall. Athene had turned her into a spider, and she immediately began to spin a delicate, gossamer web—as spiders have done ever since.

KING MIDAS
AND THE GOLDEN TOUCH

The god Dionysus is almost always shown wearing a crown of ivy and grapevine leaves, to show his close connection with wine and vegetation. He was often accompanied by the satyrs, woodland spirits who had human bodies with horses' tails and ears.

D ionysus, the god of wine and merrymaking, journeyed far and wide teaching people how to plant grapevines and make wine. Once, he lost his way and found himself in Phrygia, the kingdom of a vain and selfish man named Midas.

When Midas showed him the right road to take, the god said, "Your kindness deserves a reward. I will grant you one wish."

Greedy King Midas knew exactly what he wanted. "I wish that everything I touch may turn to gold," he said.

"Perhaps you should wish for something better," suggested Dionysus.

"That is my wish," replied King Midas.

"Then it is granted."

As he walked back to his palace, Midas absent-mindedly plucked a twig from a tree. Instantly it turned to gold. Delighted, he picked up a stone; it became a gold nugget. He looked down at his robes. They too had turned to gold. Even the path he walked on had become a golden trail!

King Midas rushed into his home. "I will drink to my good fortune!" he crowed. He sat down—on a chair that turned to gold—and ordered a servant to pour him some wine. But the minute it touched his lips, the wine turned to gold!

Worried, King Midas picked up an apple. It turned to gold before he could bite into it.

"I will starve to death!" King Midas cried. In panic, he called for Dionysus. "Help me!"

"I see you have learned your lesson," said Dionysus. "Now go and bathe in the River Pactolus."

The king did so. The river washed away his golden touch, but to this day, the riverbed glitters with golden sands.

IDUN'S
GOLDEN APPLES

Apples have a special place in the mythology of many cultures. In Greek mythology, the golden apples of the Hesperides give eternal life. In this Norse myth, golden apples give the gods eternal youth. Still today we have a folk saying: "an apple a day keeps the doctor away"!

One day Loki, the trickster god, was wandering with Odin through Midgard, the land of humans. Feeling hungry, they killed an ox and began to cook it. But the meat would not cook, even after hours in the fire.

In a tree above them sat an eagle. "If you promise to share the meat with me," he called down to them, "I will let it cook."

As soon as the meat was ready, the greedy eagle devoured it, leaving nothing for Loki and Odin. Loki hit the eagle with his staff, but it just stuck fast—and Loki's hand stuck to the staff! The eagle, who was really the giant Thiassi in disguise, flew off, dragging Loki with him.

"I will let you go on one condition," Thiassi told Loki. "Bring me the goddess Idun, and the golden apples of eternal youth that she guards." The terrified Loki agreed.

Loki went to Idun and told her he had found some apples even more wonderful than hers. "Come and see," he said, "and bring your apples, so we can compare them." As soon as Idun left Asgard, the home of the gods, Thiassi seized her.

When Loki arrived, the gods lit a huge fire. Thiassi flew straight into it. Before the eagle was burnt up, Odin seized his eyes and flung them into the sky. They shine there still, as the twinkling stars we see at night.

Without the golden apples, the gods and goddesses soon grew old and withered—and very angry! They ordered Loki to bring Idun back.

Wearing the goddess Freya's falcon cloak, Loki flew to Thiassi's mountain and found Idun. Quickly, he flew back with her to Asgard.

OLODUMARE
AND OLOKUN

Olodumare, whose name means "great everlasting majesty," was the supreme god of the Yoruba people of Nigeria. Olokun, who challenged his supremacy, is portrayed as a goddess in this story, but in other versions is a male river god.

O nce there was only water below the heavens, and the goddess Olokun was the ruler of the vast, deep waters. Then Olodumare, the ruler of the heavens and chief of all the gods, sent the god Obotala to create land on the waters. Olokun was furious. Olodumare had never told her this was going to happen, much less asked permission to disturb her watery realm.

"Why should you be the supreme ruler of us all?" she shouted up at Olodumare. "Come down, and I will prove that I am more regal, and more fit to rule over the gods!"

"I cannot be bothered with the likes of you," Olodumare replied. "But I will send my messenger, Chameleon, to see you."

Olokun fashioned a magnificent robe of deep sea blue and aqua green. She put it on, and waited for Olodumare's messenger. When Chameleon arrived, Olokun was shocked to see that his gleaming skin exactly matched the beautiful tones of her robes!

Not to be outdone, Olokun asked Chameleon to come back the next day. Then she fashioned an even more beautiful robe, of delicate shell pink. But once again Chameleon's coat matched her robe exactly.

Olokun tried again. This time she fashioned the brightest robe of all, made from fiery red coral. Once again, Chameleon's coat matched hers perfectly.

At last Olokun had to admit that she had been beaten. "After all," she said, "if his messenger is so magnificent, how much more glorious must Olodumare himself be. He is surely fit to rule over us all!"

ANANSE
AND THE SKY GOD'S STORIES

The crafty spider who outwits his opponents is a well-known figure in African mythology. The Zande people of Central Africa called him Ture; to the Ashanti of Ghana he was Ananse. Ananse stories were taken to the West Indies by slaves, and are still told there today.

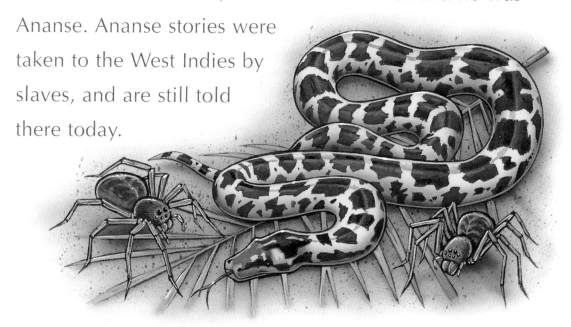

Onyankopon, the sky god, had many wonderful stories, and Ananse the spider asked to buy them. Onyankopon set a very high price. "Bring me Onini the Python, Osebo the Leopard, Mmoboro the Hornet Swarm, and Mmoatia the Spirit," he said. He was sure no one could meet this challenge, especially not a little spider. But Ananse was clever—and so was his wife, Aso.

Aso and Ananse began to cut a palm branch. As they were cutting, they argued loudly about which was longer, Onini the Python or the branch. At last Onini himself came to settle the argument. He stretched himself along the branch to show how long he was—and Ananse tied him down. So Onini was caught.

Next, Aso filled a gourd with water. "Spill the water on Mmoboro the Hornet Swarm," she told Ananse. "The hornets will think it is raining, and fly into the gourd to keep dry. Then you can trap them there." So Mmoboro was caught.

Then Aso and Ananse dug a pit between Osebo the Leopard's den and the waterhole, and covered it with leaves. The Leopard fell right into the pit. So Osebo was caught.

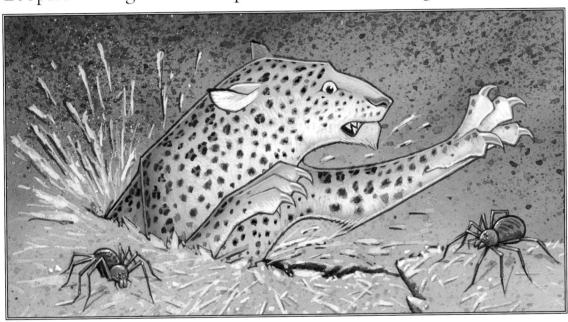

To catch Mmoatia the Spirit, Aso and Ananse carved a wooden doll and covered it with sticky tree-gum. They put the doll near a tree where the spirits played, and next to it they put a bowl of yams. When Mmoatia came by, she asked the doll for some yams. When the doll didn't answer, Mmoatia, in frustration, hit it—and her hands stuck fast to the gum. So Mmoatia was caught.

Ananse brought all his captives to the sky god. Onyankopon was pleased. "You have paid my price, Ananse," he said. "All my stories now belong to you!" And ever since then, the sky god's stories have been known as the Stories of Ananse the Spider.

Love is the most powerful emotion ever felt by many people, so it is not surprising that stories of love and marriage occur in mythologies from around the world. But these tales do not always end well. Loss and longing, two equally common and powerful human feelings, also frequently appear.

In fact, however fantastical the stories of myths and legends when it comes to love, they often reflect a deep truth about human relationships. The Greek youth Narcissus, who is too obsessed by his own good looks to notice the girl who is pining for him, struck such a chord with early psychologists that they named a state of self-obsession after him.

Myths also recognize that love is part of the whole range of human interactions. It does not only affect the two people concerned. Indeed, the Greek myth of Paris shows the havoc that results when social conventions are flouted. Helen is married to another man, but Paris still follows his heart and takes her away. As a result, the terrible Trojan War is fought, and countless men lose their lives.

In some stories, lovers are reunited in death after lives of sadness and forced separation. In these myths, faithfulness is rewarded. Perhaps the final union of star-crossed lovers represents the union with God that many people hope will happen when their lives end.

LOVE AND MARRIAGE

ECHO
AND NARCISSUS

The nymphs were woodland spirits who attended Artemis, the Greek goddess of the hunt. In some versions of this story, she is the one who causes Narcissus to fall in love with his own reflection. Someone who is vain is sometimes called a "narcissist" even today.

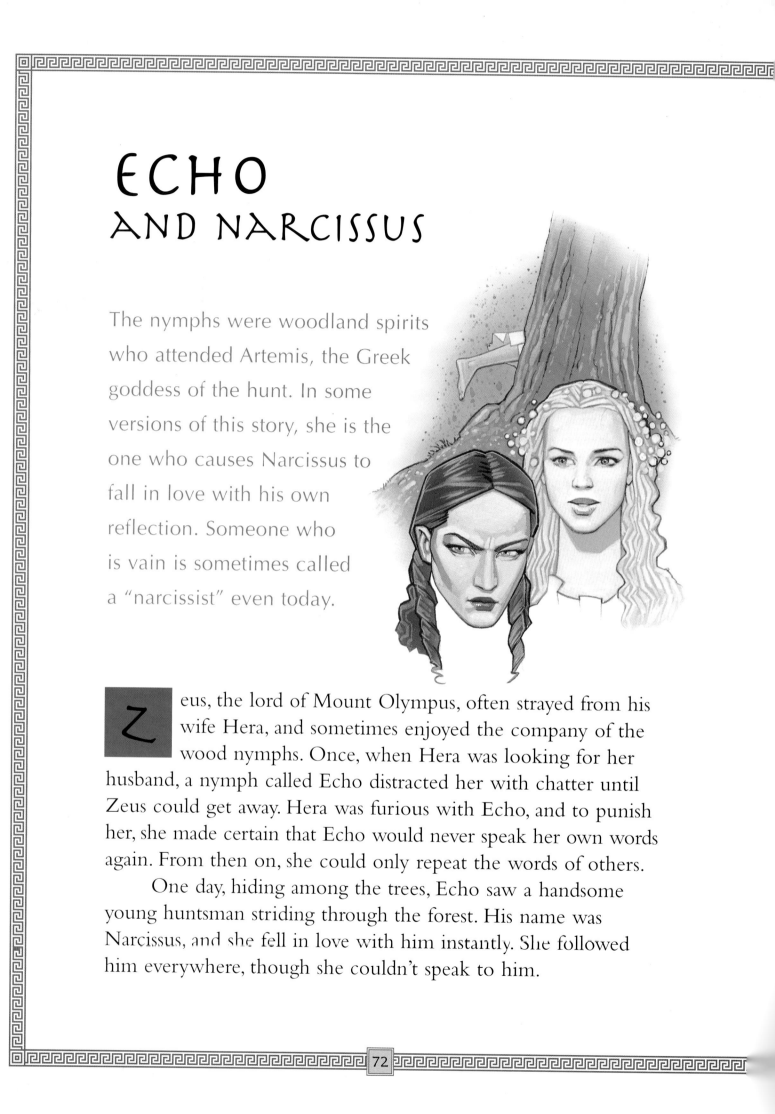

Zeus, the lord of Mount Olympus, often strayed from his wife Hera, and sometimes enjoyed the company of the wood nymphs. Once, when Hera was looking for her husband, a nymph called Echo distracted her with chatter until Zeus could get away. Hera was furious with Echo, and to punish her, she made certain that Echo would never speak her own words again. From then on, she could only repeat the words of others.

One day, hiding among the trees, Echo saw a handsome young huntsman striding through the forest. His name was Narcissus, and she fell in love with him instantly. She followed him everywhere, though she couldn't speak to him.

Narcissus, who had no interest in love, only found the nymph annoying.

"Why do you follow me?" he shouted at Echo.

"…follow me?" was all Echo could say.

"Leave me alone!" Narcissus shouted.

"…alone!" repeated Echo, her heart breaking. Unable to say what she felt, Echo grew so melancholy that she faded away into the hills, until all that was left was her voice.

The nymphs were angry at Narcissus's hard-heartedness, and they asked Nemesis, the goddess of vengeance, to come up with a suitable punishment, which she gladly did.

Nemesis caused Narcissus to fall in love with his own reflection in a woodland stream. He was so overcome with adoration that he sat gazing at it until he pined away and died. The gods then turned him into a beautiful yellow flower, which still bears his name today.

EROS
AND PSYCHE

Eros, the youngest of the Greek gods, was known as Cupid to the Romans, who often represented him as the chubby, winged cherub we see on valentines today. In this myth, however, he is portrayed as a strong and handsome young man.

T here was once a girl named Psyche who was so beautiful that she made Aphrodite, goddess of love and beauty, jealous. As a punishment, Aphrodite told her son Eros to shoot one of his arrows into Psyche's heart and make the girl fall in love with a mean and ugly man. But Eros fell in love with the girl himself. While she slept, he took her away to be his bride.

Psyche now had a beautiful home and everything she could wish for—but she did not know who her husband was. Eros never let Psyche see him—he came to her only at night, under cover of darkness.

One night, Psyche's curiosity got the better of her. She held a candle above her sleeping husband, and saw that, far from being a monster, he was the handsome god of love. But some wax, dripping onto Eros's shoulder, woke him, and he fled.

Psyche searched everywhere for her lost love. She begged Aphrodite for help. The goddess set her three tasks, the last of which was to fetch a box from Persephone, queen of the Underworld.

Psyche succeeded in her tasks, but when she got the box, she opened it. Inside was the sleep of death, and as soon as she breathed its scent, she fell down lifeless.

But Zeus, seeing all that she had gone through for love, took pity on her and had her brought to Mount Olympus, where she and her true love could be together forever.

ORPHEUS
AND EURYDICE

According to Greek mythology, the souls of the dead were ferried across the River Styx to the Underworld by an old boatman named Charon. Because Charon had to be paid, ancient Greeks were often buried with a coin in their mouth.

When Orpheus was a boy, his father Apollo taught him to play the lyre. He could coax such beautiful music from the strings that even stones danced when he played.

But music was not Orpheus's greatest love. That was the nymph Eurydice. Hymen, the god of marriage himself, came to their wedding to bless the couple. When Hymen's torch spluttered and died, and the smoke brought tears to the couple's eyes, they were too happy to take notice of this sad omen.

Their happiness remained complete until the day Eurydice was bitten by a snake and died. Orpheus's grief was so unbearable that he followed his wife down to the Underworld, determined to get her back.

No mortal had ever gone down to the Underworld and lived, but Orpheus didn't care. He played his lyre and sang of his sorrow, begging the gods to let him have his beloved wife. Hades refused, but Persephone was moved by Orpheus's music.

"Eurydice may follow you out, on one condition," said Persephone. "You must not look back at her until you are back in the world above."

Orpheus agreed, but as he journeyed back through the hushed darkness, he began to wonder if his wife was really behind him. His doubts turned to fear, then to panic, and he quickly turned—only to glimpse Eurydice's sorrowful face and her outstretched hand as she faded back into the blackness. Orpheus had lost her forever.

Orpheus lived the rest of his life in solitary sadness, his lyre still and silent with grief.

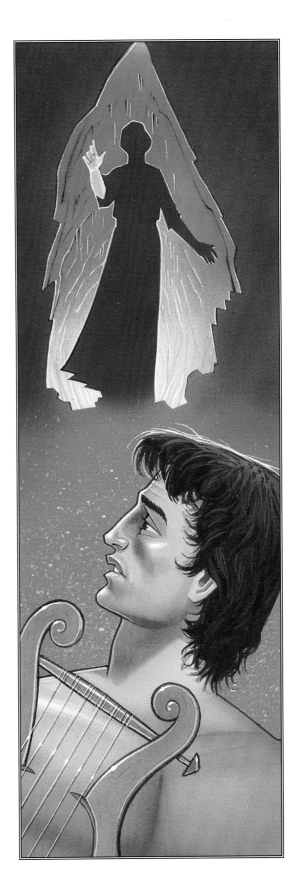

PARIS
AND THE GOLDEN APPLE

Just before Paris was born, his mother, Queen Hecuba, dreamed that she gave birth to a fiery torch that destroyed the city of Troy. In a way her dream came true, for Paris's actions in the following story led to the Trojan War.

When Zeus fell in love with the mortal woman Leda, he came to her in the form of a swan and overpowered her. She later had four children. One of them, Helen, grew up to be the most beautiful woman in the world. She married King Menelaus of Sparta, but that did not stop other men from falling in love with her. One of these was Paris, son of King Priam of Troy.

On Mount Olympus, the goddesses Hera, Aphrodite and Athene were arguing about which of them was the most beautiful. They decided to ask a handsome young mortal to decide—and the handsomest mortal they knew was Paris.

Hermes brought the three goddesses to Paris and gave him a golden apple. "Choose the fairest," he told Paris, "and give the golden apple to her."

The goddesses lost no time in trying to offer Paris bribes. "Choose me," said Hera, "and I will give you the power to rule an empire."

"I will give you the wisdom and strength to be victorious in battle," promised Athene.

Then Aphrodite stepped forward. "I will grant you the love of the most beautiful woman in the world," she said. "Helen, the wife of King Menelaus, will be yours."

Instantly, Paris gave her the golden apple.

Paris soon sailed to Sparta, where Helen, under Aphrodite's spell, fell in love with him. She returned home with him and became Helen of Troy, but Hera and Athene, still smarting with anger, made certain that Helen and Paris's happiness did not last.

DEIDRE
OF THE SORROWS

This beautiful Irish tale comes from a group of stories known as the Red Branch cycle, about the warriors who surrounded the legendary king Conchobar. One of these was Cuchulainn, who became Ireland's most famous hero.

I n the reign of King Conchobar of Ulster, the king's harper and his wife had a beautiful baby girl. There was much rejoicing at her birth, but Cathbad, the king's wise man, predicted that the girl's very beauty would be the cause of bloodshed and grief. "Name her Deirdre," he told the couple, "for it means 'sorrowful one'."

King Conchobar promised his harper that the prophecy would not come true. He had Deirdre taken away to be raised in a secret place, and he promised to marry her himself when she was of age.

But before that time came, Deirdre met a handsome young knight named Naisi, and the two fell in love. Knowing how angry King Conchobar would be, the lovers ran away to Scotland.

When King Conchobar found out what had happened, he sent a messenger to find Deirdre and Naisi and bring them home. "Tell them I forgive them and will be waiting with a royal welcome," he said.

When the messenger arrived, Deirdre begged Naisi not to go. She had had a dream in which she had seen birds flying from King Conchobar's palace with blood in their beaks. But Naisi missed his home, and ignored Deirdre's warning. He set off with her for Ulster, certain that the king would keep his word.

But instead of welcoming Naisi, King Conchobar had him killed. Then he forced the grief-stricken Deirdre to marry him. She was so unhappy that, right after the wedding, she threw herself from the king's chariot and fell to her death on the rocks below.

From the graves of Deirdre and Naisi, two pine trees grew. In time the branches stretched toward each other and mingled, growing together as one tall tree.

SAVITRI
AND SATYAVAN

This story from India is found in the Mahabharata, a 3,000-year-old epic poem that contains much of the sacred literature of the Hindu religion. The Mahabharata was originally written in Sanskrit, the language of ancient India.

Τhere was once a young prince named Satyavan, whose father went blind and lost his wealth and his kingdom. Satyavan went to live in the forest as a humble wood cutter. There he met a princess named Savitri, and the two fell in love and decided to marry.

An old wise man warned the princess not to marry Satyavan. "If you do," he said, "you will be a widow within a year." But Savitri declared, "He is my beloved, and I will have no other."

On their first anniversary, Savitri and Satyavan were walking in the forest when Satyavan suddenly fell to the ground. Savitri saw a dark-robed figure approaching, and she knew that it was Yama, the god of death.

Yama put a rope around Satyavan's neck, and took the young man away. Savitri ran after them, overcome with grief, begging Yama to take her too.

"I will come for you when it is time," Yama told her.

But Savitri kept following. "You are very persistent," Yama said. "To ease your grief, I will grant you one wish. You may have anything—except your husband's life."

Savitri wished for her father-in-law to have his sight back, and Yama agreed.

But Savitri would not leave. "Very well," said Yama. "You may have another wish." Savitri wished for her father-in-law's kingdom to be restored.

"It is granted," said Yama. But Savitri still pursued him.

"One last wish, then—and no more!" shouted Yama.

"I wish," said Savitri, "to be the mother of many children."

"Granted!" said Yama. "Now go and trouble me no more!"

But Savitri did not leave. "If I am to have many children," she said to Yama, "who will be their father? You know that Hindu widows are forbidden to remarry."

Yama was dumbstruck. Then he smiled. "Your love for your husband has outwitted death," he said. "You deserve to have him back." And he removed the rope and released Satyavan.

Savitri and her husband were reunited and lived a long and happy life together. And they did indeed have many children.

Human beings have probably always loved to hear stories of extraordinary actions and lives full of adventure. They inspire us in our own lives, and help us to feel that we can achieve more than we thought possible.

Myths and legends often tell of heroes who outwit and kill terrible monsters—dragons or dreadful creatures with several heads. These monsters can sometimes seem to represent destructive forces that people may meet in their lives, such as disease, famine, and flood. At other times, they may even appear to be like the feelings we sometimes struggle with—fear and jealousy, anger and greed.

Whatever these stories may mean, they certainly show human beings at their best. The heroes in these legends show enormous courage and skill, often managing to outwit an enemy by cunning as much as by physical strength.

In Greek mythology, Odysseus uses both to get the better of a one-eyed giant. In the Celtic legend of the Green Knight, Gawain survives because he is true to his word.

Many of these heroes are tested when they are not expecting a challenge. The stories warn their readers and listeners to be ready at all times for the difficulties life can present, but they also encourage us that the human spirit at its best can overcome almost any problem.

HEROIC
DEEDS

GILGAMESH
ENKIDU AND HUMBABA

Uruk was the largest city in ancient Mesopotamia, in what is now Iraq. Gilgamesh was probably a real ruler of this city in about 3000 BC, but over the centuries he became a legendary figure. Stories like this one were woven together into a long epic poem that dates back to about 2000 BC.

G ilgamesh, king of the city of Uruk, was part man and part god, stronger, braver and more handsome than any other man on earth. Though he was a wise ruler, he could be proud and arrogant. So the gods created another man, Enkidu, to temper his pride.

Enkidu grew up among the animals in the wilderness outside Uruk, ignorant of human ways. When he first met King Gilgamesh, he challenged him to a contest of strength. Gilgamesh won, but from then on the two men were close companions, as loving and loyal as brothers, and had many adventures together.

Near Uruk there was a cedar forest sacred to the gods, guarded by a horrible monster called Humbaba. Gilgamesh and Enkidu decided to hunt down Humbaba and kill him.

The two entered the forest, and Humbaba came roaring toward them. There was a vicious battle, but it soon became clear that Gilgamesh and Enkidu would triumph. Terrified, with Gilgamesh's sword at his throat, the monster begged for mercy and promised to be Gilgamesh's servant. Gilgamesh would have spared his life, but Enkidu grabbed Gilgamesh's sword and cut off Humbaba's head. The moment before he died, Humbaba cursed Enkidu and condemned him to die before Gilgamesh.

Enkidu and Gilgamesh paid little heed to Humbaba's curse, and began cutting down the sacred cedar trees around them. They returned home proud as heroes—but they had angered the gods, and would one day have to pay.

PERSEUS
AND MEDUSA

On his way home after slaying Medusa, Perseus rescued the princess Andromeda, who had been chained to a rock as a sacrifice to the sea god, Poseidon. Perseus and Andromeda married and became the ancestors of another Greek hero, Hercules.

P erseus was the son of Zeus and a mortal woman, Danaë. King Polydectes, the ruler of the land where they lived, wanted Perseus out of the way so that he could force his attentions on Danaë. He sent Perseus on a mission to kill the Gorgon, a scaly monster named Medusa who had snakes instead of hair growing out of her head. Medusa was so frighteningly hideous that anyone who looked at her turned to stone.

The gods quickly came to Perseus's aid. Athene gave him a mirrored shield so that he could look at Medusa's reflection instead of at her, and Hermes gave Perseus his sickle.

"It is the only blade that can cut through the Gorgon's scales," said Hermes.

To find Medusa's lair, Perseus first had to visit the Hesperides, the daughters of the night, who gave Perseus three more gifts to help him in his quest: winged sandals to help him fly; a helmet that would make him invisible; and a sack to hold Medusa's severed head. Then they told him where to find Medusa.

As Perseus flew over the island where she lived, he saw strange rocky forms—the people who had looked at Medusa and turned to stone. But he had Athene's mirrored shield, so he was not afraid. He held up the shield and struck out with Hermes' sickle, which sliced through Medusa's scaly neck as if it were a melon. He quickly stuffed the head into the sack and started for home.

Perseus returned to find that King Polydectes had treated his mother cruelly while he was away. Pulling Medusa's head from the sack, Perseus held it up before the king, and Polydectes at once turned to stone. Perseus then presented the head to Athene, who fixed it to her shield—a terrifying trophy for all time.

PEGASUS
AND BELLEROPHON

After killing the Chimera, Bellerophon and Pegasus performed many other brave deeds together. But Bellerophon grew too bold and tried to ride Pegasus up to heaven. The horse threw him and went up alone, where he became a constellation.

When Perseus slew Medusa, the blood that spurted from her neck mixed with sea foam to create a magnificent winged horse, Pegasus. Athene took the horse to Mount Helicon, where he lived wild until a man called Bellerophon needed his help.

Anteia, the wife of King Proetus, fell in love with the handsome young Bellerophon. Angry and jealous, Proetus sent Bellerophon to Anteia's father, Iobates, with a sealed letter telling Iobates to do away with the young man.

Rather than just kill Bellerophon, Iobates decided to send him on an impossible mission: to kill a vicious, fire-breathing monster called the Chimera. The Chimera had the head of a lion and the body of a goat; its tail was a poisonous snake that could kill with one bite.

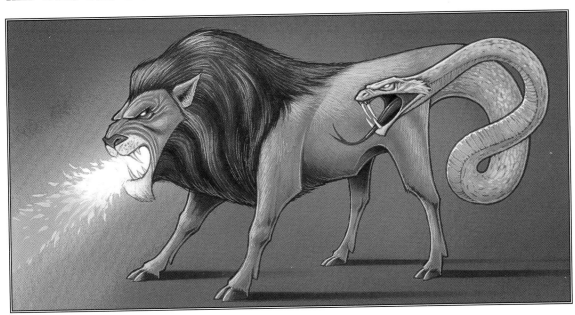

Bellerophon went to a wise old man called Polyidus for advice.

"You must tame Pegasus," Polyidus told him. "He is the only horse who can survive the Chimera's fiery breath. Go to Athene's temple and pray. The goddess will help you."

And indeed she did. Athene came to Bellerophon as he slept and gave him a golden bridle. When he awoke, the horse was grazing nearby. As soon as the wild Pegasus saw the bridle, he grew tame, and came to Bellerophon willingly. Bellerophon threw the bridle over the horse's head, climbed on his back, and rode him through the sky to the Chimera's lair.

Safe on Pegasus's back, Bellerophon was able to shoot arrow after arrow at the terrifying monster, and it soon lay dead. As a reward for his courage, Iobates gave Bellerophon half his kingdom and the hand of his younger daughter in marriage.

THE TWELVE TASKS OF HERCULES

Hercules, also known as Heracles, is one of the most famous heroes of Greek mythology. His amazing strength was obvious from earliest babyhood, when he strangled two deadly snakes that Hera put in his cradle.

Zeus often fell in love with mortal women, and one of them, Princess Alcmene, bore him a son named Hercules. Zeus's jealous wife Hera vowed to destroy the boy, but Hercules was so strong that he survived all her attempts. At last Hera asked King Eurystheus to help her.

Eurystheus gave Hercules twelve seemingly impossible tasks to perform—surely one of them would be his undoing.

The first task was to kill the terrifying Nemean lion. Hercules strangled it, and returned wearing its skin as a cloak.

Next Hercules had to kill the nine-headed Hydra. Each time one of the monster's heads was cut off, two new ones grew in its place. So Hercules set a flaming torch to the Hydra's neck each time he cut off a head. The monster was destroyed.

For his next two tasks, Hercules captured the golden-antlered stag sacred to the goddess Artemis, and the ferocious boar that lived in the mountains of Erymanthus.

For his fifth task, Hercules had to clean King Augeus's filthy stables. Hercules managed to change the course of a river so that it flowed through the stables, and they were cleaned in a day.

For his sixth task, Hercules shot down the flock of iron-clawed birds belonging to the god Ares. Then he captured a mad bull, the father of the Minotaur, and he tamed the mares of

 Diomedes, who fed on human flesh. His ninth task was to get the golden belt of Hippolyta, queen of the Amazons. After  this, Hercules succeeded in bringing back the oxen belonging to the monster Geryon.

Hercules' eleventh task was to find the garden of the nymphs called the Hesperides, and steal the golden apples that grew there. He did this with the help of the Hesperides' father, Atlas.

Finally, Hercules had to fetch Cerberus, the three-headed dog who guarded the Underworld. Hades gave him permission to take the dog to Eurystheus—who was too frightened to look at the creature! At last Eurystheus and Hera admitted defeat. Zeus was so proud of his son that he made Hercules a god on Mount Olympus.

THESEUS
AND THE MINOTAUR

Ancient vases, coins and wall paintings from Crete show many maze-like patterns, which may represent the under-world. There are also scenes of ceremonies or celebrations in which young men and women are leaping acrobatically over bulls.

When King Minos of Crete offended Poseidon, the sea god took a terrible revenge. He made the king's wife, Pasiphae, fall in love with a bull. Later, Pasiphae gave birth to the Minotaur, a terrifying creature that was half man and half bull, King Minos asked Daedalus to make a complicated labyrinth from which the Minotaur would not be able to escape. But he still had to sacrifice seven young men and seven young women each year to feed the monster and keep it content.

After nine years, Theseus, the son of Poseidon and heir to King Aegeus, decided to offer himself to the monster. He was determined to kill the creature and rid Athens of its power.

Theseus was very cunning and brave, but even he might not have succeeded if it had not been for Ariadne, King Minos's daughter. Aphrodite had caused her to fall in love with Theseus, and so she gave him a special gift. It was a spool of thread, which Daedalus, the builder of the maze, had given her.

Theseus attached the thread to the entrance of the maze and unwound it as he went deeper and deeper into the Minotaur's realm. At last he was face to face with the monster.

In a mighty battle, Theseus killed the Minotaur. Then he followed the thread through the darkness and back into the light, where Ariadne was waiting for him. Together they set sail for Athens, and Theseus's home.

DAEDALUS
AND ICARUS

Daedalus was a master inventor and craftsman whose teacher was the goddess Athene. After killing his cousin in a fit of jealousy, Icarus was banished to the court of King Minos, for whom he designed many amazing machines and buildings, including the labyrinth.

W hen Theseus escaped from the labyrinth on Crete, King Minos was so angry that he decided to punish Daedalus, the man who had built the maze. He shut Daedalus and his young son, Icarus, in a tall tower in the middle of the labyrinth.

Day after day, Daedalus and Icarus looked out of their lonely tower toward the sea. Their only visitors were the birds who sometimes came to perch on the tower walls.

These birds gave Daedalus an idea. He began gathering the feathers they shed, carefully binding them together with string and wax. In a year's time, he had made two pairs of graceful wings.

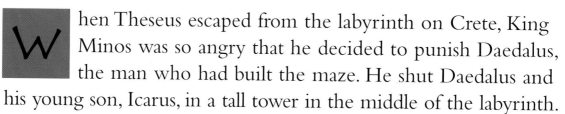

"Stay close to me," Daedalus told Icarus, strapping the wings to their shoulders. "And whatever you do, do not fly so low that the sea spray soaks the feathers, nor so high that the sun melts the wax."

Then he showed his son how to flap his arms so the wings beat the air, and the two rose up to freedom.

As the earth fell away below him, Icarus felt an ecstatic sense of mastery and wonder. Unable to contain his happiness, he soared upward, his joy expanding the higher he went.

But in his happiness, Icarus forgot his father's words. The wax began to melt, and the feathers fell from his wings. Icarus was doomed.

Daedalus watched in horror as his son tumbled down to the sea and drowned. Filled with grief, he flew on to the island of Sicily, where he built a temple to Apollo. There Daedalus hung up his wings as an offering to the god, vowing never to use them again.

JASON
AND THE GOLDEN FLEECE

In ancient Greek mythology, the centaurs were half man and half horse. Most of them were wild and savage, but Chiron was different. Wise and gentle, he had been taught by Artemis and Apollo, and in turn became the tutor of several heroes.

W hen King Aeson of Iolchos was defeated by his step-brother Pelias, he knew his son Jason was in danger. He sent Jason away to be raised by the centaur Chiron.

The time came for Jason to claim the throne that was rightfully his, and he set out for Iolchos. Along the way, he helped an old woman cross a river. She turned out to be the goddess Hera, who promised to help Jason when he was in need.

Pelias knew that Jason could destroy him, so he decided to send his nephew on an impossible mission—to bring back the Golden Fleece belonging to King Aeëtes of Colchis. This fleece was guarded by a fearsome serpent that never slept.

Jason built a magnificent ship, which he named the Argo, and set sail for Colchis. King Aeëtes, however, was not about to part with the Golden Fleece. "You must earn it," he told Jason, "by tilling a field with my two fire-breathing bulls, and planting rows of dragons' teeth."

Hera kept her promise to Jason. She caused Aeëtes' daughter Medea to fall in love with Jason. Medea helped him tame the bulls, till the field and plant the dragons' teeth. When the dragons' teeth turned into a band of savage warriors, Medea helped him defeat them.

But Aeëtes still refused to give Jason the Golden Fleece, so Jason had to take it himself. Medea helped to calm the serpent that guarded the fleece, and Jason carried it off.

Jason married Medea, and they sailed back to Iolchis to claim the throne. They hung the Golden Fleece in the Temple of Zeus, as a sign of Jason's triumph over Pelias.

THE TROJAN
HORSE

There are many stories and poems about the Trojan War, possibly based on a real war that occurred in the twelfth century BC. According to legend, the Trojan prince Aeneas survived the war, and his descendants founded the city of Rome.

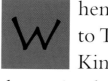hen Paris took Helen to Troy with him, King Menelaus was determined to win his wife back, so he declared war on the Trojans. He was joined by his brother, King Agamemnon of Mycenae, along with other Greek kings and generals. Armies were gathered, and ships were launched against Troy.

The Trojans had built a strong fortress to protect them against enemy attack, but they were not able to defeat the invading Greeks, who had the goddesses Hera and Athene on their side. Battles raged for years, and many men were slaughtered.

Finally, after ten years of fighting, many of the Greeks had had enough and were ready to go home. Others, however, were still hungry for victory. One of their leaders, Odysseus of Ithaca, devised a plan that could not fail.

One morning the Trojans looked out from their battlements and saw that all the Greeks had disappeared. Tents, ships, soldiers —all were gone. There was only an enormous wooden horse outside the fortress gate.

"The Greeks have finally given up and gone home!" said the Trojan generals. "They have left this magnificent horse as a peace offering!"

Only one old man, Laocoon, was wary. "We cannot trust the Greeks," he warned the generals, "even when they bring us gifts."

No one listened to him. Shouting and cheering, the soldiers opened the gates and pulled the giant horse into the city. Suddenly a door in the horse's belly burst open, and hundreds of Greek soldiers tumbled out, brandishing their spears.

The Trojans were trapped inside their own fortress by Greek cunning, and the city was soon destroyed. Hera and Athene had triumphed after all.

ODYSSEUS
AND THE CYCLOPS

This story is part of a long epic poem called The Odyssey, dating from the 8th century BC. Its author is said to be the Greek poet Homer. *The Odyssey* tells of the fantastic adventures Odysseus and his men had on their journey back to Ithaca after the Trojan War.

W hen Odysseus and his men sailed home from Troy, a storm blew them off course. They found themselves on an island, where they sheltered in a cave. Suddenly the ground shook, and in strode a terrifying one-eyed giant. He was Polyphemus the Cyclops, son of Poseidon the sea god, one of a race of giants who lived on the island. He was bringing home his sheep, and he was furious to see the strangers.

When the men begged for mercy Polyphemus picked up two of them, smashed their heads on a rock, and ate them. He rolled a rock in front of the entrance of the cave to keep the rest prisoner.

Odysseus's men were sure they were doomed, but Odysseus wasn't so easily defeated. He gave the giant several goatskins of strong wine.

"You're not such a bad fellow," slurred Polyphemus. "What's your name?"

"My name is Nobody," replied Odysseus shrewdly.

As soon as the giant was asleep, Odysseus seared a sharpened log in the fire, and drove its point into the Cyclops's eye. When the other giants heard Polyphemus howling in pain, they came running to ask what was wrong.

"Nobody is attacking me!" cried Polyphemus from inside the cave. "Nobody has blinded me!"

The other giants, thinking Polyphemus had gone mad, left him alone.

Next day, Odysseus and his men escaped by clinging to the bellies of the Polyphemus's sheep when they were herded out of the cave. By the time the giant found out, it was too late.

SIGURD
AND FAFNIR

The sword that Regin forged for Sigurd in this Norse myth was made from bits of Sigurd's father's sword, which had been a gift from the god Odin. Stories about Sigurd are also found in Germanic mythology, where he is known as Siegfried.

S igurd was a young prince apprenticed to a blacksmith named Regin. Sigurd's father, King Sigmund, had been a great hero, and Sigurd longed for adventure too. One day Regin gave him the opportunity to find it.

"Years ago," said Regin, "the god Odin killed my brother. As compensation, Odin gave my father a horde of treasure that had belonged to a dwarf named Andvari. That treasure should now be mine, but a dragon called Fafnir stole it. Kill Fafnir and bring back the treasure," said Regin, "and I will share it with you."

Armed with a gleaming sword that Regin had forged for him, Sigurd set off to find Fafnir's lair. On the way, an old man suddenly appeared before him. "Do not meet the dragon face to face," he warned Sigurd, "or his flames will engulf you! Dig a pit in front of his lair and attack him from below. Then, when you have killed him, bathe yourself in his blood. No weapon, fire, or disease will ever harm you." The stranger vanished, and Sigurd realized he had been a god in disguise.

Sigurd soon found Fafnir's lair and dug a pit as the old man had told him. When the fire-spitting dragon emerged, Sigurd thrust his sword upward, plunging it into the monster's heart. With a terrible roar, Fafnir died.

As Sigurd bathed in the blood that poured from the wound, some of it splashed onto his lips. Suddenly Sigurd understood everything the birds in the trees were saying.

"Sigurd has killed Fafnir!" they screeched. "Now Regin will kill Sigurd and keep all the treasure himself!"

So Regin had tricked him! Sigurd quickly gathered up the treasure and rode away. He went on to become as great a hero as his father had been.

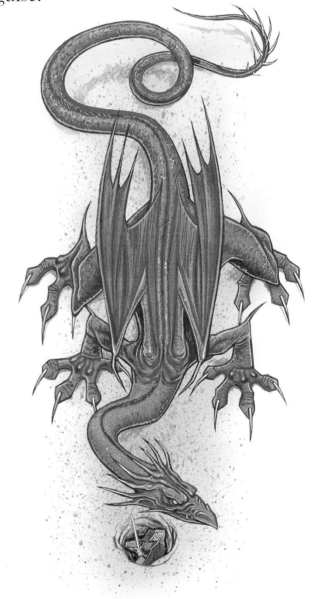

VAINAMOINEN
AND THE MAGIC MILL

According to Finnish
mythology, Vainamoinen
was the first man on earth.
He had magical powers and
was a poet and musician.
The stories of his adventures
and heroic feats have been
gathered together in an epic
poem called the Kalevala.

Vainamoinen, who was already old when he was born,
wandered the earth planting crops and trees that grew
into forests. Then he set off to the north to find a wife.

Louhi, the ugly hag who was queen of the northlands,
asked Vainamoinen why he had come. When he told her, she said,
"Make me a magic mill that gives endless supplies of grain,
money, and salt. Whoever can make such a mill for me," she said,
"will have my beautiful daughter Aino for his bride."

Vainamoinen couldn't make the mill, but he knew that his brother Ilmarinen the smith could. So he sang a wind that brought Ilmarinen to the northlands. Ilmarinen worked for three days, and when the mill was finished, Louhi was delighted. But she broke her promise, and sent the brothers away without her daughter.

Vainamoinen and Ilmarinen were furious. To punish Louhi, they stole the magic mill and sailed away with it.

Louhi sent a fog to envelop their ship, but Vainamoinen cut through the fog with his shining sword. Louhi made a fierce whale rise up from the sea, but Vainamoinen sang it down again. Louhi even sent a ship full of her helpers to attack Vainamoinen's ship. But Vainamoinen threw some tinder into the sea—it grew into a reef that caught Louhi's ship and destroyed it.

Enraged, Louhi turned herself into a monstrous eagle and flew onto the mast of Vainamoinen's ship. Vainamoinen struck her with an oar, and she tumbled from the mast, grabbing the mill as she fell. It sank to the bottom, where the grain mill and money mill were destroyed. But the salt mill is still there, grinding salt into the sea for eternity.

THE SWORD
IN THE STONE

King Arthur is one of the most famous figures of Celtic and British mythology. The story of the sword in the stone may have originated in the ancient Celtic custom of awarding the winner of a battle a ceremonial sword placed on a stone altar.

A rthur was the only son of Uther Pendragon, king of Britain. Britain was a dangerous place in those days, so the tiny prince was spirited away by the wizard Merlin, to be raised in safety by a knight named Ector. Only Merlin knew the boy's true identity.

When Uther died, the country tumbled into chaos. Tribal chieftains attacked one another and death and destruction were everywhere. A king was needed to restore peace and order.

At last the most powerful warlords decided to hold a great battle in London. The warrior who slew most of his rivals would win a sacred sword and be crowned king.

Merlin knew that a king chosen through bloodshed would only bring more bloodshed to the land. Arthur's time had come.

Taking the young boy with him, Merlin journeyed to meet the warlords. At dawn, just before the battle was to begin, Merlin addressed them.

"In the courtyard is the sacred sword that you are about to fight for. But I have put a spell on it, so that only Britain's rightful king can take it."

Everyone rushed outside. There was the sword, plunged deep into a stone on which were etched these words: "WHOSOEVER DRAWS THIS SWORD FROM THIS STONE IS THE TRUE-BORN KING OF BRITAIN."

The warriors rushed to try, but not even the strongest could move the sword. They laughed when Arthur stepped forward.

But as soon as Arthur gripped the handle, the sword slid from the stone like a knife from butter. Raising it above his head, Arthur faced the crowd.

Silently, the warlords fell to their knees. Their king had come at last.

ARTHUR
AND EXCALIBUR

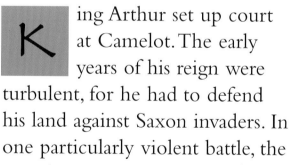

Nimue, also known as the Lady of the Lake, was said to have bewitched Merlin so that he would fall in love with her. She then imprisoned him in a wood and forced him to give away the secrets of his magic.

King Arthur set up court at Camelot. The early years of his reign were turbulent, for he had to defend his land against Saxon invaders. In one particularly violent battle, the sacred sword he had drawn from the stone was broken.

After the battle, Merlin took Arthur to a misty pool in a forest clearing, where he could offer his broken sword to the water gods, as was the custom. Arthur flung the sword's jewel-encrusted handle into the lake and turned to go.

But Merlin stopped him. There was a small boat moored at the side of the lake. "Step into it," Merlin said, "and row across."

When Arthur reached the middle of the lake, a graceful arm, clothed in shimmering white, came up out of the water. It held a shining sword and scabbard.

"Take it!" Merlin cried to Arthur. "It is yours. Take it!"

As Arthur reached out, the goddess of the lake, Nimue, rose from the water. "The sword is called Excalibur," she told the young king. "Use it wisely. With its scabbard at your side, none can harm you."

Nimue vanished, and Arthur slowly rowed to shore.

With Excalibur, Arthur was able to defend his country once again and drive the Saxons out. However, his own lords continued to fight with one another. At last Arthur gathered them all around a great Round Table at Camelot and made them vow to uphold truth and justice, and to fight only their enemies rather than each other. For many years thereafter, Britain flourished, and its people were happy.

GAWAIN
AND THE GREEN KNIGHT

The Green Knight in this story may be related to the "green man" of Celtic religion, a vegetation god who is killed at the end of summer, then is born again in the spring.

One cold night, as King Arthur and his knights feasted, the door burst open and a huge green knight rode in, carrying a mighty axe.

"I challenge any man to cut off my head," the giant cried, "if I may return the blow!"

Only one young knight, Gawain, had the courage to come forward and lop off the giant's head.

Then the giant picked up his head and rode away!

"Meet me at the Green Chapel in a year and a day!" he told Gawain.

Twelve months later, on his way to the Green Chapel, Gawain got lost in a snowstorm and sought shelter at a castle. Its lord, Bercilak, invited him to stay.

The next morning, Bercilak's wife came to Gawain's room and gave him a kiss. Gawain was surprised, but said nothing.

Later, Bercilak came home from hunting and presented Gawain with a fox. "What will you give me in return?" he asked.

To Bercilak's amusement, Gawain kissed him!

The same thing happened the next day. On the third day, the lady gave Gawain a kiss—and a green belt. "Wear this when you meet the Green Knight," she said, "and his axe will not harm you."

Later, Gawain gave his host another kiss—but not the belt.

At last it was time for Gawain to leave for the Green Chapel. The Green Knight was waiting. Twice the Green Knight swung his axe, and twice he missed. The third time, he merely grazed Gawain's neck.

"Stand up," he told the relieved knight. "It is I, Bercilak. The witch Morgana changed me into the Green Knight to test King Arthur's men. I did not strike you the first two times because of the kisses you gave me. The third time I scratched you, because you did not give me the belt. But do not be ashamed. You are an almost perfect knight."

From then on, Gawain always wore a green sash, to remind him of his amazing encounter—and that he was not quite perfect.

FINN MacCOOL
AND THE SALMON

Finn MacCool, one of Ireland's great warrior heroes, is thought to be based on a real person who lived in the third century AD. This story comes from the group of legends that grew up around him, known as the Fenian cycle.

C ool MacTrenmor of Leinster, chieftain of the warrior band known as the Fianna, died in battle. Soon after, his wife Murna bore his son, Finn. To protect the baby from her husband's enemies, Murna took him into hiding. She brought him up with the help of two warrior women, who taught the boy to be a skilled fighter.

Finn grew tall and enormously strong, and eventually the time came for him to go into the world to gain the wisdom he would need to take his place at the head of the Fianna. He sought out the poet and wise man Finegas to be his teacher.

The young man found Finegas beside a pool, where he had been trying for seven years to catch and eat the Salmon of Knowledge. The person who ate this magical fish would instantly gain the power to see into both the past and the future. Soon after Finn arrived, Finegas caught the fish and gave it to his pupil to cook.

As Finn was cooking the salmon, he burned his thumb and sucked it to ease the pain. At that moment, the fish's knowledge flowed into him, and he changed from a youth into a strong, full-grown man. Finegas knew then that it was Finn's destiny, not his own, to eat the salmon and gain its wisdom for all time.

Finn MacCool went on to become the mightiest and wisest leader the Fianna ever had, and he lived to an old age. When his days were coming to a close, it is said that he did not die, but fell into an enchanted sleep deep in a cave, where he waits to rise again one day.

A mong all the uncertainties of life, one thing is sure. Everyone who lives must die. Myths and legends have helped people to face this truth for thousands of years.

Different ways of meeting death are shown in stories from all around the world. Some characters, such as the Irish Cuchulainn, fight to the very end. Others, like Kumush's daughter in the Native American story of the Old Man and the Ancients, embrace death, going happily to meet it.

Modern medicine means that today most people expect to live long and healthy lives. Things were very different in the past. When little was understood about the human body, or the diseases that could attack it, the possibility of death was always present. Parents expected that many of their children would not live to grow up. It was rare for someone to live on into advanced old age.

Stories in which heroes met their deaths with courage helped people to feel that there were ways to triumph over the power of death, even if it would always win in the end. Many legends also give hope for the future. Even in the midst of an end as terrible as that of the Scandinavian myth of the Battle of Ragnarok, where gods as well as people will all be destroyed, there is a promise of renewal and a new beginning.

DEATH
AND
ENDINGS

GILGAMESH,
ENKIDU AND THE BULL

Ishtar, the goddess of both love and war, was more widely worshipped than any other god or goddess in the ancient Near East. In this story she is the daughter of Anu, the chief god; in other myths her parents are Sin (the moon) and Shamash (the sun).

After killing Humbaba, Gilgamesh and Enkidu returned to Uruk as heroes. Gilgamesh looked stronger and more handsome than ever, and the goddess Ishtar was overcome with love for him. She asked him to marry her, but he refused. "You have betrayed everyone you have ever loved," he told her. "I will not become one of them."

Furious, Ishtar went to her father, Anu, chief of all the gods, and asked him to make a Bull of Heaven to destroy Gilgamesh.

Anu created a ferocious bull, which Ishtar brought to Uruk. Stamping its mighty hooves, with steamy breath billowing from its nostrils, the bull lowered its horns and attacked Gilgamesh.

As Gilgamesh struggled with the creature, brave and loyal Enkidu grabbed the bull. With his bare hands, he wrestled the huge animal to the ground and tore it limb from limb. Then he and Gilgamesh sacrificed the bull's heart to Shamash, god of the sun.

Ishtar was enraged, and she cursed Enkidu. Anu was angry too, and he and the other gods decided that either Gilgamesh or Enkidu must die.

The very next day, Enkidu fell ill. Gilgamesh stayed beside him day and night for twelve days. Then Enkidu said, "I have dreamed my death. The Black Bird of Death seized me in its talons and carried me to the palace of Erishkagal, Queen of Darkness." With these words, Enkidu died.

Gilgamesh, alone with his sorrow, now grew fearful that he too would die. He wandered the earth for years, searching for the secret of eternal life. He never found it, and finally accepted that death one day comes to every human being.

THE OLD MAN
AND THE ANCIENTS

Kumush is the supreme god of the Native American Modoc people of northern California. He is said to have created the Modocs last of all the tribes, because they were his own chosen people, and he made a homeland especially for them.

Kumush, the Old Man of the Ancients who created the world, had a daughter whom he loved dearly. When she was small, Kumush gave her ten beautiful dresses, one for each stage of her life. The tenth dress was made of buckskin, decorated with sparkling shells, and it was the most beautiful of all. This was her burial dress.

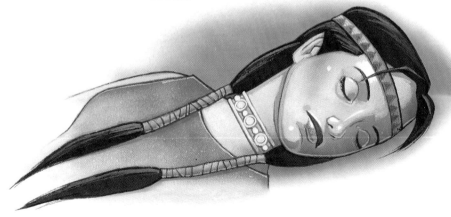

One night, just before she became a woman, Kumush's daughter dreamed that she would die soon. The next morning she asked her father for her burial dress. Kumush offered her all the other dresses, but she wanted only the buckskin dress with the bright shells. As soon as she put it on, she died.

Kumush was so grief-stricken that he followed his daughter down into the Underworld, where the spirits live. There he saw more spirits than there were stars in the sky, more than the hairs on the head of every person on earth. The spirits danced, and Kumush danced with them. They danced for six days and six nights, and when they stopped, the spirits became dry bones.

Kumush put the spirit bones in a basket and took them back to the world above. When he was back in the sunlight, he scattered the bones on the soil, and they grew into all the tribes of humankind.

Then Kumush and his daughter journeyed west along the sun's road to the middle of the sky. They live there to this day.

THE DEATH OF
KING ARTHUR

The mythical island of Avalon, King Arthur's final resting place, was the place where the sword Excalibur was said to have been forged. It was probably related to the ancient Celtic "otherworld" known as the Blessed Isles, but it has also been associated with Glastonbury in Somerset.

Arthur had ruled Britain for many years, and had driven out the Saxons. Now he faced a new enemy. His nephew Mordred wanted to take over the throne, and had declared war on the king.

On a field near Camlann, Arthur's and Mordred's armies met. A fierce battle raged for hours, until at last Arthur and Mordred were face to face. Mordred attacked, plunging his sword deep into Arthur's stomach. Arthur knew he was finished, but with his last ounce of strength managed to lift his sword Excalibur and cleave Mordred's skull. Then he fell to the ground.

Bedwyr, one of Arthur's warriors, rushed to his side.

"Bedwyr," gasped Arthur, "I am dying. Throw my sword into the river as an offering to the water gods."

Bedwyr took the mighty Excalibur to the riverbank, but he could not bring himself to throw it in. When he returned to Arthur, the king told him to go back to the river and do as he had asked.

But Bedwyr still could not bear to throw the sword away. Only when Arthur told him a third time did Bedwyr cast the sword into the river. He was astonished to see a white-sleeved arm rise from the water and catch it.

When Bedwyr returned to the spot where Arthur had been lying, the king was gone. Turning, he looked out to the river, and saw a black barge sailing away with the king's body lying on it. "Do not be afraid, Bedwyr," whispered a woman's voice. "We are taking Arthur to Avalon, where he may rest for all eternity."

The barge sailed into the distance, and Arthur was never seen again. But some say that one day he will return, when Britain needs him most.

CUCHULAINN
THE WARRIOR

Cuchulainn, Ireland's most renowned hero, was the central figure in the legends known as the Ulster cycle. The goddess Morrigan, who was with him when he died, sometimes appeared as a warrior in battle, but most often took the form of a bird flying over the battlefield, screeching to warn of coming death.

Cuchulainn, the Hound of Ulster, was descended from gods and wise men. When he was a small boy, it was predicted that he would become a famous and mighty warrior, but that he would die young.

At the age of seven, Cuchulainn was so strong that he killed a huge, fierce dog by smashing it against a stone. By the time he was a young man, he was the greatest warrior in the army of King Conchobar of Ulster.

When Queen Maeve of Connaught sent soldiers to steal the precious Brown Bull of Ulster, King Conchobar's army was under a spell that made the men too weak even to lift a spear against the invaders. Only Cuchulainn had escaped the curse, and he faced Queen Maeve's army alone. Single-handed, he sent the army fleeing back to Connaught.

Cuchulainn fought heroically in many more battles against Ulster's enemies. Then one day, on his way to battle, he saw one of the fairy folk weeping as she washed some blood-stained clothes in a river. He knew that the clothes were his, and that she was weeping because he was about to die.

But Cuchulainn didn't turn back, and he fought his last battle as bravely as his first. Even as he was dying, Cuchulainn refused to lie down. Wounded and bleeding, he strapped himself to a standing stone in the middle of the battlefield. There the war goddess Morrigan, in the form of a crow, sat on his shoulder as he was dealt his death-blow.

The mighty Hound of Ulster died young, as the wise man had predicted, but his fame continues to this day.

THE BATTLE OF
RAGNAROK

This Norse myth describing the terrifying battle that ends the world, carries within it the hope of renewal. Lif and Lifrasthir—whose names mean "life" and "eager for life"—are not just the last man and woman on earth. They also become the first people in the new world that rises from the old.

L oki, the mischievous, trouble-making god, caused many calamities for the gods of Asgard. Of these, the most terrible was killing Odin's son Baldur the Beautiful, the god of light. All the gods of Asgard rose up in fury against Loki. He tried to escape their terrible anger by hiding away in the mountains, but the gods found him and bound him in chains, with a serpent above him, dripping venom onto him. There Loki remains to this day. His wife Siguna catches most of the venom in a cup, but every now and then a drop hits Loki's face, and he thrashes and howls. Then the whole earth trembles.

But one day, after three terrible, fierce winters pass with no summer between them, Loki's son, the wolf-monster Fenrir, will release his father from his chains, and Ragnarok, the final battle, will begin. Fenrir will devour the sun and the moon, the stars will tumble from the heavens, and lightning will shatter the sky. The rainbow bridge that joins Asgard to Midgard will burst into flames, and Loki and the Fire Giant Surt will lead the giants into battle against the gods. Surt will set the world ablaze, and all the warriors—gods as well as giants—will perish in the flames. Only Odin's son Vidar, who will slay Fenrir, will survive.

One human couple will survive, too—Lif and his wife Lifrasthir, who will take shelter in the branches of Yggdrasil, the world-tree. When the battle of Ragnarok is over, they will climb down, ready to bring life and hope to the world once more.

INDEX

Actaeon (Greek) 58
Aeëtes (Greek) 96
Aegeus (Greek) 94
Aeneas (Greek) 100
Aeson (Greek) 96
Agamemnon (Greek)100
Aido-Hwedo (African)14
Aino (Norse) 106
Alcmene (Greek) 92
Amaterasu (Japanese) 36, 54
Amulius (Greek) 48
Ananse (African) 68
Andromeda (Greek) 88
Andvari (Norse) 104
Anteia (Greek) 90
Anu (Mesopotamian)118
Aphrodite (Greek) 22, 74, 78
Apollo (Greek)32, 76, 98
Arachne (Greek) 58, 60
Artemis (Greek)58, 72, 98
Arthur (Celtic)108, 110, 112, 122
Aske (Norse) 24
Aso (African) 68
Athene (Greek) 58, 60, 78, 88, 90, 96, 100
Audumla (Norse 24
Baldur (Norse) 126
Bedwyr (Celtic) 122
Bellerophon (Greek) 90
Bercilak (Celtic) 112
Bestla (Norse) 24
Bor (Norse) 24
Cathbad (Celtic) 80
Cerberus (Greek) 92
Chameleon (African) 66
Chaos (Chinese) 16
Charon (Greek) 76
Chimera (Greek) 90
Chiron (Greek) 96
Co-chin (Native American) 50
Conchobar (Celtic) 80
Cool Mac Tremnor (Celtic) 114
Cronus (Greek) 20
Cuchulainn (Celtic) 80, 124
Daedalus (Greek)94, 96
Danaë (Greek) 88
Demeter (Greek) 44
Dionysus (Greek)58, 62
Ea (Mesopotamian) 28
Echo (Greek) 72

Ector (Celtic) 108
Embla (Norse) 24
Enhil (Mesopotamian)28
Enkidu (Mesopotamian) 86, 118
Epimetheus (Greek) 22
Erishkagal (Mesopotamian) 118
Eros (Greek) 74
Eurydice (Greek) 76
Eurystheus (Greek) 92
Fafnir (Norse) 104
Faustulus (Greek) 46
Fenrir (Norse) 126
Finn MacCool (Celtic) 114
Gaia (Greek) 20
Gawain (Celtic) 112
Geb (Egyptian) 10
Gilgamesh (Mesopotamian) 86, 118
Green Knight (Celtic) 112
Hare (African) 34
Hecuba (Greek) 78
Helen of Troy (Greek) 78, 100
Helios (Greek) 32
Hera (Greek) 72, 78, 92, 98, 100
Hercules (Greek) 88, 92
Hermes (Greek) 22, 88
Hesperides (Greek) 88
Hippolyta (Greek) 92
Homer (Greek) 102
Horus (Egyptian) 56
Humbaba (Mesopotamian) 86, 118
Hymen (Greek) 76
Icarus (Greek) 96
Idun, goddess (Norse) 64
Iobates (Greek) 90
Ishtar (Mesopotamian) 28, 118
Isis (Egyptian) 30, 42, 56
Izanagi (Japanese) 36
Jason (Greek) 96
Kumush (Native American) 120
Laoco\on (Greek) 100
Leda (Greek) 78
Lif (Norse) 126
Lifrasthir (Norse) 126

Loki (Norse) 64, 126
Louhi (Norse) 106
Maeve (Celtic) 124
Manitou (Native American) 48
Mars(Greek) 46
Medea (Greek) 98
Medusa (Greek) 88, 90
Menelaus (Greek) 78, 100
Merlin (Celtic) 108, 110
Midas (Greek) 58, 62
Minos (Greek) 94, 96
Minotaur (Greek) 94
Miochin(Native American) 40, 50
Mmoatia (African) 68
Mmoboro (African) 68
Mordred (Celtic) 122
Morrigan (Celtic) 124
Murna (Celtic) 114
Naisi (Celtic 80
Nanu-Buluku (African)14
Narcissus (Greek) 72
Nekumonta (Native American) 48
Nemesis (Greek) 72
Nimue (Celtic) 110
Numitor (Greek) 46
Nut (Egyptian) 10
Obatala (African) 12
Obotala (African) 66
Odin (Norse) 24, 64, 104, 126
Odysseus (Greek) 102
Olodumare (African) 12
Olokun (African) 66
Onini (African) 68
Onyankopan (African) 68
Orpheus (Greek) 76
Orunmila(African) 12
Osebo (African) 68
Osiris (Egyptian) 42, 56
Ovid (Roman) 58
Pan Ku (Chinese) 16
Pandora (Greek) 22
Paris (Greek) 78, 100
Pasiphae (Greek) 94
Pegasus (Greek) 90
Pelias (Greek) 96
Persephone (Greek) 40, 44
Perseus (Greek) 88, 90
Phaeton (Greek) 26, 32
Polydectes (Greek) 88

Polyphemus (Greek)102
Poseidon (Greek) 88, 94, 102
Prometheus (Greek) 22
Proteus (Greek) 90
Psyche (Greek) 74
Ra (Egyptian) 10, 30, 54
Regin (Norse) 104
Remus (Roman) 46
Rhea Silvia (Roman) 46
Rhea (Greek) 20
Romulus (Roman) 46
Satyavan (Indian) 82
Savitri (Indian) 82
Sebek (Egyptian) 56
Set (Egyptian) 42, 56
Shakok (Native American) 40, 50
Shamash (Mesopotamian) 118
Shanewis (Native American) 48
Shu (Egyptian) 10
Sigmund (Norse) 104
Siguna (Norse) 126
Sigurd (Norse) 104
Sin (Mesopotamian)118
Spider (African) 34
Surt (Norse) 126
Susanawo (Japanese) 36, 38, 52
Tefnut (Egyptian) 10
Theseus (Greek) 94, 96
Thiassi (Norse) 64
Thoth (Egyptian) 56
Tsuki Yomi (Japanese)36
Tulugaak (Inuit) 26, 38, 54
Uke-mochi (Japanese) 40, 52
Uranus (Greek) 20
Uther Pendragon (Celtic) 108, 110
Utnapishtim (Mesopotamian) 26, 28
Vainamoinen (Norse)106
Ve (Norse) 24
Vidar (Norse) 126
Vili (Norse) 24
Yama (Indian) 82
Yggradisil (Norse) 24
Ymir (Norse) 24
Zeus (Greek)22, 72, 78, 88, 92